BOOK DOCTORING NUTS AND BOLTS

Your Manuscript Is Ready to Go:

Now How Do You Get It Ready for Publication?

(with some extra help on getting to the finish)

Kathy Tuten, B.A., M.ED

Contents

The Emotional Stuff

The Art (and Work) of Getting Published

Lessons from my writing class, each of whom has a great book in the works and finally got to the point that they had the *what* and the *so what* and now needed the *now what:*

Mina Bell – memoir

Barbara Frazier – memoir/biography of her mother

Dianne Hull – mystery

Dorothy Pike – mystery

Leslie Wilson - biography

Introduction

OK. You're well into your manuscript, several chapters, or even close to the finish, or you think you're finally finished.

And you've just about decided, "Hey! This is good stuff! I think this is even worth trying to get published!"

You've had friends read your manuscript to get some idea of whether it's really as good as you think it is. And they say, "Go for it!"

And your kids have read parts, or your spouse has read through pretty much the whole thing, and even your spouse says it's good stuff. (Whoa! Really? How unexpected!)

Or, you're pretty happy with what you've got so far, but you're bogged down somewhere in the middle.

Or you've got some serious writer's block.

Or one of your characters doesn't seem to be going anywhere.

Or the middle of your story is really mushy for some reason.

What's up with that? What do you do now? How do you fight through to the end? Well, I've got some ideas.

And once you get everything squared away, you get to a good ending, you reunite the hero and heroine after many obstacles, your detective finally finds the perpetrator of the gruesome crime, your archeologist finally unearths the fabulous lost treasure, your memoir is up to date, your biography completely covers the part of your person's life that you wanted to cover.

Even though the writing may have bogged you down in some places you've just about done it. You have a completed manuscript ready for public consumption.

But now what do you do???? Well, I've got some suggestions!

This handbook will help bridge the gap between your completed manuscript and the wonderful reviews your published book gets from book reviewers.

This handbook will explain all those things that no one tells you you need to do and those things about book publishing you didn't know you didn't know.

This handbook is designed to help you get through the rough spots with some concrete ideas for how to handle:

- Frustration
- Writer's block
- Mushy middles
- Descriptions: the downfall of lots of writers – either too much or too little
- Writing dialogue
- How to set up a writing group
- How to make sure your manuscript is 'cleaned up' and ready for an agent or for publication
- How to know when you're really ready to publish
- What steps to take to get your manuscript ready for an editor or an agent
- How to get an agent
- Whether or not you need a professional editor and what one does
- Self-publishing vs. major book publisher
- On line tools for help with everything from outlining and notecards to the actual uploading for self-publishing.
- Web sites that could prove very useful to you at each step of the publishing process

There are four sections to this handbook:

1. Pulling it all together
2. The nuts & bolts of editing and proofreading
3. The emotional stuff
4. The art of getting published: publisher or self-publishing?

There is lots of 'white space' where you can actually make notes to yourself and have them all in one place so you don't lose track of any of them.

There's also a Check Sheet at the back of the handbook to help you get yourself organized.

This is kind of the down and dirty, the most basic information to get you on the road to publication, whether you go the major publisher route or you decide to self-publish. It's not intended to be an encyclopedia but it *is* intended to get you moving forward and getting your book to the audience you have intended to read it.

Putting It All Together

What's It All Mean?

Before you go any farther with your manuscript do a gut check.
You're pretty well satisfied with your manuscript but before you even think about submitting it to a publisher or an agent, ask yourself a few really important questions.

Think about the following questions and then jot some notes to yourself.

1. What's more important at this point: you loving the story/plot in your manuscript or other readers loving your plot/story?

2. How many times should you read and reread parts of your manuscript before you decide it's ready for publication? Why?

3. Is there a difference between your manuscript being totally "done" and your manuscript being "good enough to publish"?

4. Is there any place in your manuscript that you tend to skip over when you're rereading? If so, why? If so, that's a red flag!

5. What's the best part of your manuscript? Why do you pick this part? What can you translate from this really good part to another place in your manuscript you're not so thrilled with?

6. What part would you change if you had more time and energy and talent? Why? So why not do it?

7. How many people do you know personally who would pay $25.00 to read your book?

8. Do you work best in the morning, the afternoon, or at night? This might seem like an irrelevant question at the moment, but if you're trying to power through a writing session to the end of your manuscript every morning at 9AM sharp and you're not really making much progress, why are you doing that if you're really a night owl????

9. How many times do you think you should revise your manuscript before submitting it for publication? Why?

10. How will you know when you're finally through with this plot?

These are good things to think about as you get to the end of your book, especially if this is your first one. So how are you feeling now?

Seeing is Believing

All good writers want their readers to be able to "see" where the actions of the story take place. Good writers have the ability to create story settings that make the reader believe what he's reading. The questions an author needs to be able to answer are: how do you want your readers to feel? To see? To hear? For example: do you want the reader to be afraid, happy, sad, or sorrowful? So think about a scene you remember from a book that you liked. It could be outside or inside, a small room or a big area. Think through what you can remember.

❖ What book is the scene from? Who's the author?

• What are the colors in the scene?

• What did you "see" first in the scene?

• What did you "hear" first in the scene?

• What did you "smell" first in the scene?

- What was the time of year of the scene? The season? The weather?

- What was the time of day of the scene? How did you know that was the time of day?

- What kinds of physical objects, "props," were in the scene?

- What character or characters were in the scene? Name each one, if you can, and describe each one in a sentence or two.

- How was – or were – the characters feeling during the scene? How did you know?

- What can you take away from this exercise that will help you with your own descriptions?

I will tell you that descriptions, both long and short, ae critically important to a good book. So we'll work a bit on those.

Descriptions of Scenes

Before you try to revise and edit on the large scale – the story plot as a whole – take a look at the one place that sinks an otherwise good book, the one thing that will get you turned down by a publisher before your manuscript even gets a complete reading.

Writers are sometimes stymied by descriptions of places or people. The most common mistake writers make is not describing *clearly enough.* That doesn't mean describing till the point your readers fall over from boredom. But it really helps your readers if you can give them a mental picture of what your characters look like and where they are in the world.

We are a very visual society so you need colors plus smells and noises and tastes. It really helps, if your main character works in a big city, for example, to describe what's going on around her: the sounds of the subway, the smell inside the local coffee shop, the smell of leaves on the ground in October, the colors of the table at Thanksgiving, the colors of the skyscraper lights at the holidays.

Try this exercise to help you make sure you are getting all you can out of your descriptions. Find a couple or three photos that you really love. They could be photos you've taken or could be from a book or a magazine.

1. Look carefully at each photo you've chosen. Where are you? What state? What country? What town? What part of the world?

2. How do I as a reader know where you are (physical place)? What identifying characteristics can you give me in writing? Or if you don't want me to know where we are yet, what clues can you give me that will help me 'solve' this mini-mystery eventually?

3. What happened here just before you got here? How do you know?

4. Describe the scene. **However,** you may NOT use the following adjectives:
    a. Pretty
    b. Green
    c. Red
    d. Yellow
    e. Pink
    f. Purple
    g. White
    h. Brown
    i. Black
    j. Beautiful
    k. Dark
    l. Light

You MUST use alternate adjectives for your description. While this might seem like a not very useful activity, trust me, you'll learn a lot of good alternative words to use instead of those old trite ones. If you get stumped get online and find a good thesaurus, or go buy an inexpensive one. They are wonderful for a writer to have around.

Go for it!

Describe Scene 1:

Describe Scene 2:

Describe Scene 3:

5. Think of *three* similes you can use to describe each scene (a simile uses the word 'like' or 'as.') Examples: He was blind as a bat. The clouds looked like whipped cream. He's as prickly as a porcupine when you cross him.

Scene 1:.

Scene 2:.

Scene 3:.

6. Think of *three* metaphors you can use to describe each scene (a metaphor uses the verb 'to be.') Examples: He is a raging lion when he's angry. He is our very own Santa Claus.

Scene 1:.

Scene 2:.

Scene 3:b.

Note: similes and metaphors are extremely useful as you try to describe characters and scenes so your readers will be able to picture what you're talking about. Your aim is to have them feel like they are there, like they are right in the scene with your characters. One caveat: although we use both similes and metaphors every day without even thinking about them, just don't get carried away. Too many can end up boring your readers.

7. What do you think is going to happen five minutes after you leave this scene?

Scene 1:

Scene 2:

Scene 3:

8. What else can you tell me about this scene?

Scene 1:

Scene 2:

Scene 3:

9. Now think: can you translate one or more of these scenes into your own novel/memoir/biography/autobiography to make it better? Why is this scene important to your story as a whole?

Just remember: good descriptions fit their circumstances and don't give away the whole plot at the beginning of the story. They don't overkill and they don't leave the reader saying to himself: whaaaaat? You might go through what you've got on paper so far and look out for the 'yucky' places: those descriptions that you read over again and think, "What in the world was I trying to get across here?" Or, "Oof; this is too much!" Or, "I really have no idea what this character is like as a person; I didn't do him justice on paper." Those are the places in your manuscript that you need to help with some really good description.

You might want to do this particular exercise with any of the scenes or characters in your own plot that you have decided you're not all that happy with, or maybe they don't tell us as much as you would really like to tell.

If you're writing a memoir or autobiography you still need to write dynamic descriptions of the situations you found yourself in and the people and places you met along the way.

If you're writing a biography or about a certain period of history you need to keep your readers' interest by writing clear descriptions of the real people and places you're covering. What were people eating every day in the 15th century? What medical techniques existed during the reign of Henry VIII? Who were the political people circling around your character in the 18th century Especially if you're writing about a person many of us might not like or identify with (Hitler, Charles Manson, the Unabomber) you need to make us really 'see' this person and the circumstances around him/her that have caused him/her to be worth the time it took you to write about him!

As you go back through your completed manuscript take a look at people and scenes that leave you kind of bored, or just not interested. You can punch up these scenes or character descriptions very easily by adding some creative description.

Jot some notes to yourself about a scene or a couple of scenes you feel could use some help.

List the page number and the paragraph number and maybe make some quick notes about exactly what you don't like, and a few thoughts/words about the change.

And In the End

Beginnings of a story are really easy to write; you've got the idea, you can see the plot almost all the way through and you're excited to be writing. Endings sometimes get short shrift from writers because the writer has known what's coming, so it's not as exciting to write about. Or you've gotten so far into your story that you suddenly realize you don't have a clue how to tie up all those loose ends! Or where some of your secondary characters disappeared to.

Beware: you don't want to leave your readers unhappy at the end of your story because then they won't read your second story. So you need to think a little about the end of your book: how do you want to structure it? It *does* need structuring; wonderful endings don't just fall off the turnip truck. You need to make sure you've got a good one, a thorough one, a powerful one.

Fear not: here are some ideas. If you're stuck for an ending, go back and read through what you've got so far and think about which of the possibilities below best fits your characters. You might already have one of these endings below in mind for your ending. If so, feel good about it. If not, there's hope yet.

There are many ways to end your story, whether it's fiction, biography, or memoir.

1. Everybody wins. In this ending the hero/heroine comes out on top, solves all problems, and, as far as we know, lives happily ever after. Secondary, or supporting, characters end up happy as well. Everyone gets married at the end, or wins the gold medal, or finds the treasure, or gets the fortune from Grandma.

2. Big party. This ending describes a big celebration, at least for the main characters. That could mean a big wedding celebration, or election celebration, or the recovery of the stolen emerald. But it's a BIG celebration. And it might leave room for a sequel, but it doesn't have to.

3. "Never-ending Story." We all know by the end of your story what's going to happen next, but you fade out before we actually get that far. This is a good ending if you think you might write a sequel to your first plot. We don't actually *know* what lies beyond the sunset that the hero and heroine ride off into, or what the sunset looks like. This leaves you room to keep these characters alive beyond this particular story.

4. Full circle. You bring your main characters back to where they started in the first place. But because at least your main character has grown considerably – emotionally, intellectually – this ending highlights a major difference in your main character. A sort of 'before and after,' if you will. Your main characters have learned some kind of lesson, one that might leave them older but wiser, or better off, or worse off. But they are back to their regular routines even if those routines have changed somewhat. This ending is really an ending. So this particular main character is pretty much through. This is finality.

5. Riding off into the sunset. For this ending you really wrap up the whole plot a bit before you get to the final scenes. So your detective solves the crime – perfectly – gets the girl – perfectly – and then you describe how the two of them ride off into the sunset, literally or figuratively. But before they do you have recapped for us how the crime was solved, or how the two main characters got together, or how the hero found the huge diamond, so they can, in fact, ride off together with nothing hanging over their heads. This is kind of the 'Perry Mason Effect', where he explains all the clues that led him to his verbal attack on the man on the witness stand, and the witness ends up crying and confessing right there on the stand. But the falsely accused is immediately exonerated and leaves the courtroom with the love of his life.

6. Main character wins, but comes out the other side damaged or broken. The quest has been so fierce, physically, spiritually, or mentally that the hero has no more energy left at all. He has gone far beyond what was expected and done a great service, perhaps, but there are no more emotional dollars in his account. Many 1930s 'noir' novels *started out* with an emotionally broken hero; think about *'The Maltese Falcon'* or *'The Postman Rings Twice.'* The fascination to readers was to see if the hero could actually pick himself up enough to carry out another mission.

7. Unresolved ending. This ending may serve your purpose if you have a situation in which one or more of the characters has suddenly been cut off – murdered, jailed, lost, disappeared, because you can't figure out what to do with him. Or if his disappearance throws a wrench into the solving of the crime, or the heroine's dream of marriage. Or if the readers never learn which one of two main villain characters actually committed the murder. This ending does not resolve the main conflict of your story and it may leave the reader hanging. You may want your ending to leave an open question if you want to come back around to this character or situation in a later story. But be aware that most readers want some kind of closure. They don't really like to be left hanging with a 'What's next' or a 'Wait a minute, what happened here?'

8. "Smashed fourth wall." For this ending you step outside the fictional narrator's voice and speak to your readers directly, as the author of the narrator. Confusing? The 'fourth wall' is the imaginary barrier you've designed that keeps the characters in your story from knowing they're characters in a story. In other words, your characters think they're real and act as if no one is watching them. So at the end you might say something like, "Dear reader, you know that Mary is going to go right back into another disastrous relationship...." Or think about a story like *'Sex and the City'* in which Carrie Bradshaw moves the narrative along by voiceovers, speaking directly to the viewers what she's thinking and feeling. There's also a set of famous fictional detectives who work in the "Peculiar Crimes Unit' of the London Police Department. They are always in trouble. And in <u>The Burning Man </u>the narrator says, after describing the chaos in the unit, "welcome to the offices of London's Peculiar Crimes Unit. For the sake of succinctness this account will be trimmed off......." The narrator is speaking directly to the reader to let the reader in on the 'joke' as it were.

Your particular plot line, fiction or biography or memoir, will probably tell you which ending you need. By the time you get two-thirds of the way through your plot you'll have an idea if you want to finish off this plot for real, or if you already have a sequel in mind, or if you want to send one of your secondary characters off on an adventure of her own.

What you really want to do is offer your readers some sort of closure. Remember that people generally like to fill in the holes in the circle or the square; we just do it automatically. We want some kind of very clear indication of what has happened and why it happened in the way it did. And many of us want to go beyond that into what we think might happen in the future. And especially with mysteries and adventure stories we all love to get a sense of satisfaction from making the clue connections, even if we didn't figure it all out till the very end.

How do you know if you have the right ending? *Read it out loud!* If it doesn't really grab you, try one of the three alternate endings you've come up with (next exercise). Which one sounds the best? The most logical? That's the one you want!

Endings

Write three very different endings for your story. No kidding...... And if you're having some difficulty deciding exactly how you want to end your plot this might very well give you the 'aha moment' you needed. Who knows, you might discover the idea for your second novel!

1.

2.

3.

Use some scrap paper or open a new document on your computer. Why do this? You can just jot down a few sentences, and you may open up some thoughts about pulling your plot together that you hadn't thought about. And, you might end up with the *beginning* of another plot line

The Problem of the Ugly Middle

The middle of your story is what makes your book work. The beginning and the end are critically important, and truly define your story, but you need to get from that beginning to the end somehow with some kind of logic. And you need to keep your readers interested enough to get to the end!

What you need to think about after you get your wonderful beginning down on paper:

1. You need to introduce your first dramatic complication to your plot not too many pages in. Something to consider: without at least a couple of plot complications and twists your story might be over in 25 pages. Do you want that? Plot complications keep readers just off balance enough to want to find out what happens next. *That's* what you want, right? This is the point at which the heroine has met the love of her life, but the first plot twist is beginning to step between her and her true love. Or the point at which the hero of your mystery first discovers that his best friend might have been the person who actually committed the murder. Have you done that? What's an example? What's an incident you particularly like? How can you throw in a complication at that point?

2. You need to gear up the tensions between characters, and conflicts between them. You need to throw in some really good and really appropriate conflicts between or among people. And some conflicts between scenes. "Conflict" doesn't necessarily mean physical confrontation. Guns or knives or fists or bombs may be true plot points in your novel but a good conflict may simply be an argument over dinner by your two main characters, or a dark stranger crashing your heroine's party, or a suspicious noise outside your window at midnight. Have you done that? Where?

3. All the way through the middle of your plot you need to occasionally throw in a conflict or a complication here and there. These are conflicts that can be at least partially solved before the next 'mini-conflict' happens. The tension rises and falls throughout your plot as it leads up to the big ending. Have you done that? Where? What's a good example that you really like?

4. Add some conversations between and among your characters to 'show' what's going on rather than telling so much. You may have gotten bogged down in way too much description/narrative without making anything sound interesting or exiting or disturbing or horrifying or...... Have you done that? Example? Where is a conversation you've drafted that you really like?

5. As you get to the point in your story where you begin to see the ending you might want to throw some seemingly insolvable problem right in front of your heroine. Think about Indiana Jones and the snakes: seemingly insurmountable but.... Something tbhat occurs toward the end of the middle of your story, right before you begin to pull all the threads together. Did you do that? What is it?

What to Do to Keep the Middle from Crashing

How does the middle get mushy in the first place and what can you do about it?

1. The middle of the story may be much less interesting to actually write than the beginning or the end. The beginning is fresh and exciting and the ending is all wrapped up in a bow. So as you write, and you begin to feel like you're slogging through a lake of mud, just keep remembering how good you'll feel when you finally solve the puzzle at the end. So don't give up, keep writing tight prose.

2. You haven't really planned how you're going to get from the beginning of the story to the ending. If you haven't figured out at least some kind of general mapping of your plot you may end up getting yourself confused, or suffer from writer's block, or get lost in all the possibilities of where you can take your plot. By the middle of your story you may have so many paths in front of you that you don't know which one to choose. So drop back a bit and think about your plot from beginning to end. Where are you intending to go with this story?

3. It will really help if you plot out some of the possibilities before you get swamped.

    - A plot outline is a wonderful thing to have before you even start writing.

    - A character outline can help you keep your characters from mushing into one another, keep them separate and ensure that your readers understand the differences among them.

    - I know it sounds old-fashioned but some kind of outline, even if it's just words and phrases, can remind you where you're going and where you've been.

    - So if you haven't done an outline by this point jot down some notes to yourself of what your major plot points are: what the four or five major events should be in your plot. No more than that: you'll just confuse your readers.

    - Then you can double-check yourself on the boring (not many, we hope) parts of your middle.

    - It's never too late to make some kind of simple outline to help with your memory. It could be as simple as:

Character 1-protagonist	Character 2-antagonist
Motivation:	Motivation:
Where did he start out in this plot:	Where did he start out in this plot:
What does he do first:	What does he do first:
What does he do next:	What does he do next:
How does he solve his major problem:	How does he give himself away:
And so on	

4. A tip: put the description of each of your characters on a note card: get the big 5x8 ones so you can describe to your heart's content.

- Put each of your major scenes on a separate note card. That way you can move characters around if you need to or move scenes around.

- Or you can decide that the brown hair you've given to one character really fits better on a different character.

- These cards can also help you to decide that you really don't need that character or that particular scene.

- So you can solve some problems of your mushy points very easily by just deleting them completely or moving them to a whole different place in your manuscript.

- Problem solved! Or you can save those characters or those scenes for your next novel!

- So:

Character's Name:
How tall:
What complexion:
Daily routine:
Normal job:
Bad habits:
Good habits:
Likes to eat:
Lives in:
And so on.

5. One caveat: although it's a really good idea to have more characters at your disposal than you might need, just don't fall so in love with each of them that you feel compelled to include them somewhere in the plot. A lesson: *Game of Thrones,* which is an incredible story line but some people say they get confused by trying to keep track of so many main characters that they get frustrated with the whole thing. No one will ever quit watching if they truly love the program, but if you're just starting out, you don't want to confuse yourself by including too many major characters. You also don't want to confuse your readers so much they quit reading….

6. You find that you, yourself, are bored with the plot at this point. So sit yourself down and think it through. If you are bored, then your readers won't follow you to the end of the story. What generally happens here is that writers get stuck in a 'this happened, then this happened, then this happened' mode. That will just increase your own boredom, and farewell to readers. The hard part: cut out the boring parts completely if they don't move your plot along, or at least shorten them. So you'll need to back up to the individual parts that bore you and think hard about either doing some rewriting or just simply cutting them out. You can always save them for a later novel, so don't cry too hard over your cuts.

7. Remember that one of your best plot points for a boring section or muddled section is a new complication or a new plot twist, something to throw your main characters off a little, and throw your readers off, maybe happily. So throw a wrench into the works somewhere that doesn't seem all that interesting to you. You'll find you inject interest immediately into your plot and your readers will keep reading.

8. Go back and look at your main character(s). Put them into some kind of situation where the reader thinks they'll never make it through! It doesn't have to be a life or death situation, but something just nasty or awful enough to be fun to write and to jolt your readers out of their complacency. Think about Indiana Jones or …….

9. Drop a few clues into a couple of situations near the middle of your story about what may be coming up to perk up your readers and make them say, "Uh, oh, I'm not sure where we're going here….this could get really interesting." This is the equivalent of the *Jaws* music that frightened the heck out of everyone because as soon as you heard it you KNEW something bad was coming but not what... So you can do the same thing with words if you think about it. Or perhaps the scene in the horror movie when the heroine decides to open the closet door and you just KNOW what's going to happen.

10. I've talked to a number of writers of fiction who also do 'scene cards.' They tell me that scene cards that they draft sometimes before they get too far into their plot help them when they are stuck in the middle of the plot and they think that moving the action from one place to another might solver their mushy middle problem quite easily. They also tell me that they use locations they've been to and love, or have seen in movies and love even though they've never been there or sometimes even places they've seen that they hope never to see again. Again, if you want to do those get some 5 x 8 cards and jot down some things like:

- Where is this? Country/city/forest/beach….where?

- What's the weather?

- What's the season?

- What things are in the scene? As in: beach chairs/wooden deck/country store/subway station/city street lamps….what?

- What natural things are in the scene? Rhododendrons/blue mist over the mountains/sea shore of pink sand….what"

- What colors are in the scene?

- What do you hear in the scene?

- Are there any other people in the scene?

Writing Dialogue

Now take a look at the other major problem that will quickly sink your manuscript: poor dialogue.

Writing dialogue doesn't come easily to everyone. So if you're uncomfortable with writing dialogue yourself don't feel compelled to fill your plot with it just because you think you have to. Ernest Hemingway's *The Old Man and the Sea* has no real dialogue, after all, and it's still a classic.

Good dialogue can help you move your plot along and give us, the readers, clues as to what's going on with your characters, or clues about what *could* be coming. It can sometimes take the place of pages of description or narration that would otherwise bore us right out of finishing your book. Bad dialogue, or stilted dialogue, or even poorly punctuated dialogue can turn a reader off completely.

So here are some points of reference to get you past your first discomfort with writing dialogue.

1. When you're out in public, listen to how other people talk to each other. Sit down in a public space in your local mall. Listen for expressions people use more than once when they're talking. Listen for speech rhythms and cadences as they talk. Listen for figures of speech they use more than once in conversation. Pay attention to the natural pauses in the conversations you hear. Take some notes for future reference. Your fictional characters might really be able to use some of the things you hear just in passing. You can use a little tape recorder or your phone to catch some real-people dialogue if that helps you remember what you've heard. (Just be careful here if you choose to do that.....)

2. But dialogue isn't exactly the same as real people speaking. Because remember that you can give us clues about what each character is thinking, which we would probably never get from a conversation in real life. But it should *sound* like real speech as much as you can make it sound. However, be aware that 'recording' an entire conversation between two of your characters or even several of them together would probably be crushingly boring after a couple of minutes. So as you write dialogue think about 'filler words' you've used: 'uh' and 'um' and 'I think' and 'you know' and 'like.' Edit out the pieces of dialogue that don't really seem essential, that don't move your plot forward. Think: unless it's essential for us to know, we only really care that your detective's daughter wore a red sequined dress to her dance last night because we care about him and his family (whom you've already described), and we sure don't want to hear it described sequin by sequin in a conversation with your detective's partner. A little of that kind of dialogue can really add to our picture of your characters but a little goes a long way.

3. Don't give away the plot too early and too thoroughly all at once. Don't make it obvious to us that we're being fed information. Put conversations where they make sense to you, little bits at a time if necessary. Think: if a conversation doesn't sound logical to you after you reread the whole scene throw it out! Don't tell us everything right at the beginning of the story, even if you're writing a memoir. You can trust your readers to remember important details from previous conversations earlier in your story.

4. Break up your dialogue with physical action. A long conversation with no action on the part of your characters will get boring fast. Remember that your characters are supposed to be real people with real ways of moving and acting and reacting. And some physical description in and around your dialogues breaks up what could be boring. Talking heads on every three pages won't get your readers very far. People in real life move around while they're talking to each other. Pay attention to physical gestures which will make the dialogue more interesting: the chain smoking, the nervous leg jiggling, the chewing on fingernails, the picking up and putting down of knick knacks, the aimless wandering around the room. Attention to these kinds of details can give readers clues about what's going on beneath the surface of the dialogue, clues we might really appreciate.

5. Don't overdo what are called 'dialogue tags,' unusual or weird ways of saying, essentially, 'he said' or 'she said.' Sometimes getting too cutesy with tags can detract from what is otherwise your brilliant dialogue. That being said, here's a list of words you might not have thought of to use in place of 'he said' or 'she said.'
   - Acknowledged
   - Admitted
   - Agreed
   - Answered
   - Argued
   - Asked
   - Barked
   - Begged
   - Bellowed
   - Blustered
   - Bragged
   - Complained
   - Confessed
   - Cried
   - Demanded
   - Denied
   - Giggled
   - Hinted
   - Hissed
   - Howled
   - Interrupted
   - Laughed
   - Lied
   - Mumbled
   - Muttered
   - Nagged
   - Pleaded
   - Promised

- Questioned
- Remembered
- Replied
- Requested
- Roared
- Sang
- Screamed
- Screeched
- Shouted
- Sighed
- Snarled
- Sobbed
- Threatened
- Warned
- Whimpered
- Whined
- Whispered
- Wondered
- Yelled

6. Be very careful of stereotyping any of your characters and then creating dialogue to reinforce the stereotype. Watch out for dialogue that might depend, you think, on your character's country of origin or race or ethnic origin, but which doesn't seem realistic as you reread.

7. Use profanity sparingly.

8. Use slang terms sparingly. In real life there are actually very few people who talk only in slang and who use profanity-laden figures of speech constantly and consistently.

9. Pay attention as you read other people's writing to what kinds of dialogue you think might work for you, or won't work for any of your characters. Think about when you got really sucked into a character and what he or she was going through and you couldn't put the book down. On the other hand, when did you stop believing in a character? Did good or bad dialogue help you believe or make you turn away from a character, or characters? Which writers do you read regularly that you really identify with? Who writes wonderful dialogue, to your way of thinking? What's a bad experience you've had with dialogue writing that turned you off? That means dialogue that doesn't suit the characters in some book you've read; some character talks silly, or abusively, or strangely for the circumstances. If a character in something you've read doesn't seem to make sense when she's talking you know the writer is in trouble with you! Therefore, you want to try *not* to make the same mistake....

10. Make sure any dialogue you use suits each character. It doesn't make much sense if you're writing about a detective in late 18th century France to be using 21st century technology terms. Particularly if you're writing historical fiction, check your dialogue periodically to make sure it fits the time, the place, and the character. It also doesn't make sense if you're writing a rags to riches story for your street urchin to be using words that would come out of a Wall Street broker's mouth, at least till the urchin gets rich and famous.

11. Punctuate dialogue correctly. After all, you want your readers to get lost in your plot, and not get lost wandering around in your poor dialogue. And trust me, bad punctuation will get to you every time.

12. One of the nice things about the use of dialogue is that it can provide what's called 'white space' on the page. That is really what it sounds like: empty space on a page. Through the use of dialogue at strategic points in your plot you can give your readers time to think through points you're trying to make through your characters' conversations. So if you're having some trouble getting your dialogue to suit you try writing a conversation on every other 'line' to see if that will make your characters seem more real. You don't have to leave it like that in your final version, but that extra spacing might really help you to focus the dialogue.

Why Do You Need Dialogue Anyway? What Does Dialogue Do?

1. It enables you to *show* your reader what has happened, in addition to just telling.

2. It adds some drama to what might otherwise be a very mundane piece of your story.

3. It helps you recreate an incident in someone's life that you may see differently from others you know. In other words, it tells your side of the incident: what 'really' happened, if you're writing a memoir or an autobiography. If you're writing a novel, dialogue between your main character and other characters in your story can help move your plot along without pages and pages of description. There are some things and some people in your story that you probably can't describe enough but sometimes a quick injection of a conversation about what's going on in your characters' lives may be all you need.

4. Dialogue can change the flow of your story. If you've been doing straight narrative for a while, some dialogue can serve as a good 'illustration' of what your narrative is about. Some dialogue in the middle of a long stretch of story-telling can change the pace of your narrative. In other words, it can shake up your story so you keep the interest of your readers.

5. Dialogue can help set a mood for an incident in your story: is the situation really happy, sad, distressed, confusing, joyful? Is your main character a really serious, hard-nosed type of person who has a really soft side buried somewhere deep? All you need is a quick conversation between him and his least-favorite co-worker about his favorite niece or his rescue dog to get that point across.

6. Dialogue can convey information to your reader very concisely. Where you could be wandering around for pages in narrative, a good dialogue can give your reader the exact information you were wanting him to get in the first place. Dialogue can sometimes reveal to your readers what you want them to know about a character that you can't get across as well with description.

7. Dialogue can add some color to your story. Think about creative conversations, even colorful vocabulary used by some of your characters. Expletives are not generally wonderful at any point, but sometimes you need a character that uses very colorful language as part of his personality.

8. Dialogue can help your reader understand the character of your characters (!). Your reader can use your dialogue to judge your characters and make kind of informed decisions about whether he likes or dislikes a character, whether he trusts or distrusts a character. Especially if you have a character that often expresses very profound thoughts you might want to get those thoughts into a dialogue format. Or if you have a character that frequently says funny things or off the wall things get those things into dialogue so your readers can really appreciate them.

9. Using dialogue strategically can give your reader clues about what's coming in the action of your story. You can offer clues and hints about what your character is up to. You can foreshadow where your story is going without giving away any information you're not ready to disclose.

10. If you're writing an autobiography, biography, or memoir, dialogue can help you fill in missing or sketchy details about an incident perhaps long past that people can't remember very well. If you're writing straight fiction the sky's the limit on what words and how many you put into your character's mouth. With the true stories, keep the dialogue as close to the truth as you can, only filling in details that make sense to you so you can move the action along.

Writing Dialogue Practice: A Little Reminder

If dialogue writing is not your thing, a little practice might help you feel more secure.

Think for a couple of minutes about two of the main characters in your story.

Use two of the characters you've created for your story for each of these exercises.

1. Write a scene of dialogue that creates tension between your protagonist and a supporting character when they first meet.

    Character 1:

    Character 2:

    Situation:

    Conversation: (use some scratch paper if you need to)

2. Write a scene of dialogue where your villain (antagonist) reveals an important clue to your protagonist.

    Villain (name if we know him yet or some sentence he leaks in a conversation that will give us a clue as to who he is, if we're paying attention):

    Character 1:

    Villain:

    Situation:

    Conversation:

3. Write a scene of dialogue where a supporting character tells your protagonist something that will change the course of your protagonist's actions or how your protagonist proceeds.

Protagonist:

Supporting character:

What does the supporting character reveal:

Conversation:

4. Write a scene of dialogue that shows how one of your supporting characters and your protagonist interact with each other. Keep in mind that the relationships between and/or among your main characters need to change somehow over the course of your story, for good or ill. Characters need to learn about each other; if they live and work together for some time in your story their relationship is bound to change. If it never gets beyond "Hello, how are you?" you will lose your readers eventually, because all our relationships in real life morph occasionally in good directions or bad ones. So think about your characters and their complicated relationships with the people closest to them.

Protagonist:

Supporting character:

Their relationship at the beginning of the story:

Their relationship as the story moves along:

Conversation now:

5. Write a scene of dialogue that shows the true relationship between your protagonist and your antagonist.

    Protagonist:

    Villain: (remember – we readers won't see this so no spoiler here)

    Conversation:

6. Write a scene of dialogue that reveals a plot twist! Please, please make the plot twist logical to your readers, even if they don't see it till the end of the story. You want them to say to themselves either "Aha! I knew it!" Or "Rats! I should have seen that coming!"

    Who:

    Situation:

    Big plot picture:

    Twist:

    Conversation:

OK, now plug one of those dialogue scenes into your own plot. See how easy that is?

Punctuating Dialogue

When you are writing dialogue, you really need to pay attention to at least some of the more standard conventions of punctuation. I've already said that poor dialogue structure will kill you with readers, so practice to get it right.

1. Use correct paragraphing. You begin a new paragraph on the page each time a new character speaks, or each time one character responds to another character.
   For example:
   "Why am I not believing nobody's home?" Bettina said.

   It was freezing standing there and I had already had enough waiting. I was going down the list of residents' name cards, pressing each button one after the other.

   "I hate when they make us do this. If anyone answers, you up for talking?"

   "Why me?"

   "You're smarter. Wait, no, that can't be it."

   "Funnier, too," she said.

   (from The Hunt Club by John Lescroart)

2. Always put terminal punctuation – commas, periods, question marks – inside the quotation marks.
   For example:
   Right: "I wonder," she said, "if Mary will join us after all?"
   Wrong: "I wonder", she said, "if Mary will join us after all".

3. If you interrupt the dialogue in mid-sentence, then the second part of the quote starts with a lower-case letter. (see # 2 above) If you interrupt the dialogue at the end of a sentence but you pick it back up in a sentence or two, you need to start the new sentence in the quotation marks with a capital letter. Look at #1.

4. In the case of a 'speech within a speech' you use double quotation marks on the outside of the whole speech and single quotation marks to indicate that there is a thought expressed within a larger thought.
   For example:
   "Mrs. Palmer," Hunt said, "when the Manions adopted Todd, when they first brought him home, do you remember anybody remarking on the fact, the strangeness of it? I mean Carol was fifty-six or fifty seven, and you said to her, if I remember correctly, 'Carol, you already have a seventeen year old son. What do you want with a baby now?' Do you remember asking her that?"

5. Show how your characters react to one another or feel, either toward one another or even just in general, by using dialogue to help define their physical movements or reflect their voice quality and their personality.

   For example: He said quickly, "I... am the one who stole the TV. Arrest me now!"
   Or:
   The words poured out of him like melted chocolate. "*I am the one who stole the TV. Arrest me now!*"

   She was very sad. She said quietly, "I will miss you."
   Or:
   She turned away from me. Her voice was barely audible. "I will miss you."

   Do you see how the second example presents the same information as the first example, but makes a more dramatic, effective statement?

6. In this day and time, some well-respected authors don't use quotation marks at all. Sometimes they just start a new paragraph of dialogue without any quotation marks. Or sometimes they start each new 'speech' with a dash at the beginning of the line. If you only have two characters talking back and forth to each other for a brief conversation, you don't necessarily have to use quotation marks at the beginning of each new paragraph. However, until you get used to writing dialogue, I would if I were you. Or until you write your first best seller and everyone knows who you are.....

7. The use of dialect in most novels, or even nonfiction, for that matter, can be quite controversial. You will need to make a decision regarding dialect of one of your characters if she is Scottish, for example, or Irish, or a native French speaker. My rule of thumb is that you should probably avoid putting all but the most important words and/or phrases in dialect. There are occasions when too much dialect can make the story line confusing for the reader, if he can't figure out what your character is trying to say. So just use the occasional word or phrase to reflect the fact that your character was born and raised in the backwoods of the Appalachians. You want your readers to identify with your character, so a little dialect might be really good, but if the character never speaks in anything but dialect, that gets old fast. If you feel you need to use some particular dialogue that is local to a small place in the world, go ahead and use it, but what you can do is have your non-dialect characters 'translate' the dialogue to each other in plain English. For example, by replying to the character in Standard English your readers will pick up the dialect through the context of those responses. Working their explanations into a conversation will keep your dialect from detracting from your story and may very well make your readers enjoy the conversations more.

8. Keep sentences in your dialogue as brief as possible. That means lots of s-v-o sentences: subject-verb-direct object. Those are called simple sentences, and you can rearrange words within your sentences to keep them from getting totally boring. When you get into compound sentences, complex sentences, and compound-complex sentences you may lose some of your readers, who have trouble wading through the verbiage. If you think about it, most of us do speak out loud in simple sentences. We're trying to get across our point to fellow conversationalists. That usually means we don't speak in long, convoluted phrases and sentences. So take a lesson from real life.

9. If at all possible, write in the active voice, not the passive. That means: "He read the book with much enjoyment," not "The book was read by him." Passive voice indicates that actions are being done *to* someone or something. You want your readers to feel a part of the action of the story, so you need to keep your verbs in the active voice as much as possible.

10. Avoid overuse of adjectives and adverbs in conversations. Stringing long lists of either in a sentence just overwhelms your plot. Choose adjectives and adverbs wisely: using fewer and bolder of both will help your readers see a more vibrant picture of the scene or character you're explaining to them.

11. Frequently, you can solve your adverb/adjective problem if you figure out some really powerful nouns and verbs to use instead of the old trite ones we're all familiar with. Replacing a tired old descriptive noun with a fresh one that catches your readers up in your description may mean you don't even need a string of adjectives in front of it at all. Go back to page 29 ????? to look at all the possibilities for replacing the word 'said' and then check out a good thesaurus for some noun replacements where you feel your point is not getting across as well as you'd like.

A few places you might want to look for help, or reinforcement or just double-checking your dialogue, your punctuation, your spelling are:

- Strunk and White, <u>The Elements of Style</u>
- William Zinsser, <u>On Writing Well: The Classic Guide to Writing Nonfiction</u>
- Mark Lester and Larry Beason, <u>McGraw Hill Handbook of English Grammar and Usage</u>

The Nuts and Bolts of Editing and Publishing

The next step in the process is editing: your own editing once you feel your manuscript is complete, and/or perhaps a professional editor if you decide you need one.

There are five basic kinds of editing

Continuity editing

Structural editing

Style editing

Story editing

Line editing.

But not to worry! They kind of fold in on themselves, so you can do more than one kind of editing at the same time in a reading of a manuscript.

So… While your imagination is running like a new Ferrari, go with it. Don't worry about editing.

My rule of thumb is: get it down on paper first and then worry about correcting or amending or cutting or revising.

But when you get to a logical stopping place go back and reread at least a little. Do it chapter by chapter or section by section. Don't try to mark up page by page. At least not yet. That kind of editing – line editing – can come much later. Right at the moment you want to make sure your whole manuscript holds together well without any holes.

Let's start with the big picture: continuity editing.

Continuity Editing

Look back at your manuscript. You may have a finished version, or you may only be into it a few chapters. What you're looking for here is a straight flow of your plot outline. Continuity editing makes sure your story line goes in a sensible order from one plot point to the next. You want to make sure transitions from one section or chapter of your story to the next section or chapter are logical; you don't want your readers to get lost between Chapter 3 and Chapter 4. So you need to look out for places where you find yourself saying things like, "Wait, what?" or, "OOPS, where did that come from?"

Continuity editing takes into account that you may have several places where you've thrown in a plot twist or a plot complication, or you've introduced a new character that the reader wasn't expecting but you need in order to move your plot forward. But the plot needs to keep moving in one direction only. You don't want it wandering around from place to place or character to character for no good reason.

You might also want to give your manuscript to a good friend to read and answer the following questions for you. Now is *not* the time to get worried about what someone else will have to say; any suggestions they might offer are worth your taking a look at before you try to get your book published.

1.   What is especially effective about this draft? What do you remember most from it?

2.   How well organized is the draft?

3.   Are there any places in the draft that need additional details or examples? If so, jot down the page number, or maybe page number and paragraph number if it's mostly just one or two paragraphs that have you concerned.

4.   Is there enough action, enough story, or should the writer (you?) supply more information in this draft? Suggestions?

5.   Does the story flow? Can you follow it, or are there places where you get lost? Where are these? Again, jotting down page numbers would be a help to the writer. Use some extra scratch paper if you need to.

6. Watch out for places that jump around too much. One chapter ends in Hong Kong and the next one starts out in Kansas City. How in the world (no pun intended) did we get here? Are there any of those disconnected sections?

7. Does the writer (you?) use description, dialogue and sensory verbs? Where should there be more? Does the writer both 'show' and 'tell'? If the writer is doing too much telling and not enough showing, point out two places that could easily be improved with descriptive language. Give the page number and paragraph number.

The main point here is to make sure the whole plot makes basic sense to you - no illogical surprises, disjointed plot points, new characters appearing or familiar characters disappearing half way through your plot.

Structural Editing I

Structural editing makes sure that your plot doesn't take too many twists and turns. Or leave big holes in your story line. Or put too much information into one section and skimp completely on another section.

This is where you might think of the 'skeleton' of your story. You know that a skeleton holds the whole body together; without a skeleton most living creatures would just sort of collapse in on themselves and probably die. The same with your story line. If your plot structure doesn't hold together your whole story will die and readers will lose interest when it does. While continuity editing focuses on chunks of the story holding together, structural editing looks at the big picture.

Take a good look at your manuscript.

Dig out a piece or two of scratch paper or open a new folder on your computer to hold some notes.

1. Is the beginning interesting? What makes you like the first several paragraphs?

2. Does the narrative start with action (dialogue, interpersonal interactions)? Jot down several sentences from the beginning of the manuscript that illustrate good action of some kind.

3. Does the manuscript, as far as it goes, tell a story? Does it have a beginning, a middle, and an end? Keeping in mind that the manuscript may not be finished, can you begin to tell where the story is going? How can you tell?

4. Are there any flashbacks so far? If so, do they help move the story forward?

5. What sensory details can you find? Jot down a few that you find really good. Can you see major scenes in your mind? Hear what's going on? Smell the surroundings? Taste the coffee? Feel the sand running between your fingers as your heroine digs up the corpse on the beach?

6. Do you feel transported to the place and time where the story is happening? Jot down a few phrases or sentences that help to transport you.

7. How is the dialogue so far? What's good? What would you change, if anything?

8. Do you feel that you are getting to know the characters? Do you care about the main characters? What descriptions or dialogue make you care about the characters?

9. Is the 'villain' of the story well enough described that you can dislike him? Can you see where he's coming from (or where he *thinks* he's coming from)? In other words, can you tell what his motivation is?

10. Does the main character seem to be learning something from the forward motion of the story line? What is the main character learning about other characters? About himself? About his place in the world?

11. How is the pace of the story so far? Any places that seem to be bogged down? Any places that seem to be racing forward so fast that something important gets lost or goes missing? List page numbers and examples here.

12. Does the ending, so far, provide a sense of closure to you, the reader?

Structural Editing II

Once you've got a nearly completed manuscript, you're up to more than one chapter, you might want to work on the following revisions.

1. Take *one* chapter of your manuscript – just do this for one chapter, not all of them - and look at each paragraph in that chapter. Write the purpose of that paragraph just in a word or two in the margin. (Examples: explains motive; sets up murder; sets romance in motion,)

    a. Afterwards, go back and see how much redundancy you've got from paragraph to paragraph to paragraph. In other words, are there four or five (or more) paragraphs that are pretty much saying the same thing over and over? Do you need all those paragraphs?

    b. Also look for what's missing. Do you have a scene, for example, in which the heroine of the story is kidnapped and was spirited from one moving car to another, but we didn't hear how that happened? Go back and add to your narrative if you need to, just to clarify.

    c. What did you learn that you can use in looking through your other chapters?

2. Take a section of your narrative that you're unhappy with for some reason, a piece of your story that doesn't seem to be working.

    a. On a separate sheet of paper write a note to yourself: Dear Self, what I was trying to do in this section was_____. Go back and look at that section to see if you really did what you wanted to do.

    b. On your note to yourself write down what you like about this section. Be honest here, you must have liked something, since you wrote it in the first place.

    c. Point out to yourself where you think you're holding yourself back.

    d. Write down what you can do to develop the 'bad' spots to make them better.

    e. Then make a list – bulleted is easy to reread later – of specific things you can do to improve that section. This could be as simple as: needs more color words (since the action is taking place inside the big tent at the circus); or, as complicated as: need to rethink this whole confrontation since I can't remember why I chose to use knives (as the weapons)....

3. Then ask yourself, and, again, think about this for a few minutes: why am I hung up on this part? What do I need to do to fix it? Or do I need to throw the whole section out and start over on that part?

4. Look through your manuscript and find a chapter or a section that doesn't jump out at you, that doesn't have what's called the 'wow factor.' An easy fix for this situation is to add a whole new character to it and then write some dialogue between your main character and that new character. By 'new' character I don't necessarily mean toss in someone we've never heard of before. Add a new scene between characters we've met, maybe a conversation they haven't yet had but they should have that will move the plot along.

5. Go through your manuscript and look at the scenes you have already written where characters are interacting with each other in conversation. If you think a scene like that one could use some improvement get into each of your character's heads. Ask yourself:
   a. What does each character want from this conversation?
   b. What's the risk to each character from this conversation, good risks and bad risks (hint: think adding some foreshadowing)
   c. What is each character NOT saying to the others? That information could be as important to your plot as what they are saying out loud to each other. Unless you're writing in 1st person, and that means we can only see inside your main character's head, and that's very hard to do, we can see what your characters are thinking as well as what they're saying out loud.
   d. What is the real function of this scene? What purpose does it serve in the grand scheme of things in your plot?
   e. After you've rethought, rewrite the dialogue to punch it up, or write dialogue if you don't have any in the first place.

6. If you've gotten several chapters into your story, close up your manuscript and write the back book cover text for the story.
   a. This is a teaser for your readers on what your book is about, to make them want to buy your book.
   b. Your summary shouldn't be any longer than 125 words.
   c. Think about this: if you can't get it into 125 words, you're still struggling with your point of view. You don't know where you're going, or you don't have your whole plot clear in your head. So you need to really think it through.

7. If you're still at loose ends at this point, just put your manuscript down for a week and come back to it. You know you're ready to go back to it when you can't remember all your plot points. That makes it feel new (or at least refreshed) when you go back to it, so you will have a revised or even new perspective on it when you go back to it.

Structural Editing III

Here's an exercise you can do as you work through your manuscript. Ask yourself the following questions about any character you've designed, any scene you've written, or any whole chapter.

1. Does this character, scene, chapter advance the plot any? It's important that your plot keep moving forward from episode to episode. Keep a watch out for characters you've introduced that eventually seem to go south on you: they don't seem to be adding anything substantive to the plot. If that happens cut them out or rewrite their actions so they *do* add to the forward movement of your plot.

2. Does the character reveal the motivation you want it to reveal? We all want to see why your characters do what they do. Remember that what motivates your characters, the good guys or the bad guys, is important to your plot. You don't want a 'silly' motivation – like one of your main characters slashed another one just because he didn't like her spaghetti sauce - to show up in the middle of your story. That will turn off your readers.

3. Does this character or scene or chapter give your readers important, relevant information? Remember to explain why your characters think the way they do, why they do what they do, why they say what they say. Don't let your chapters get too sidetracked from the major points you're trying to make. There's a whole series of good mysteries that features a caterer who just happens to be friends with a police detective and invariably gets involved with helping him solve his cases, so sometimes she puts recipes and menus in the middle of chapters to reflect her catering business, a plot device which really adds to the story by showing how she's smarter than the detective she works with (which we already suspected anyway). But in other words, unless your plot is centered around someone with a special talent that somehow connects to your basic plot line leave out the recipes.

4. Does this passage really characterize the main character? Have you given enough information about your main character? Or have you left out something major? Did you forget to tell us that your detective is a recovering alcoholic who is trying to make up for lost opportunities? Does your narrative reinforce what you want us to know about this character or do you find that you've gone off sideways somewhere in the middle of the passage? Do we really need to know that your character loves bacon cheeseburgers? Or that she hates frilly dresses? Just think it through……

5. Does this character or scene or chapter increase an existing conflict you've got going, either good or bad? Does it create a new conflict, or mini-conflict? A 'good' conflict could be tension between two characters that works to the good of the plot, e.g. the hero detective falling in love with his female suspect but he certainly can't let on to anyone he knows.

6. Does the plot overall play on our senses in a good way? Do you think we can see into the scene and hear and feel and smell? Remember that vivid imagery puts a picture in our minds, which is what we want. We want to feel as if we're right there with your characters.

7. Check to see if your main characters, especially, are static or dynamic. If characters don't learn as they go along in your plot we readers will lose interest in your story. A static character isn't worth our time or energy. A static plot is not worth reading. That would mean, for example, that your detective hasn't got a clue, literally, about how to solve the crime and that he just stumbles onto the answer to the mystery. All your major scenes and conversations need to radiate with energy. If you go back and read through some of them and they seem static to you, you need to rewrite, or at least revise. If you're old enough to remember TV detective Columbo, think about how he always looked like a bumbling fool but he kept pushing and pushing and pushing until he got the true bad guy, so *we* knew even if no one in the story knew there was method to his madness.

8. Are your characters and scenes honest? True to themselves? How will we readers know that they are being as honest with themselves as they can be? This is especially important if you're writing a memoir or a biography or an autobiography.

9. Is there a 'moral' to your story? If so, how will we recognize it? Remember, readers love to see the hero succeed and the bad guy get his comeuppance.

Lines, Sentences, Words – Line Editing

Now that you've got your plot and your big picture point set, let's look at some of those little nit-picky things that will do your book in if you're not careful. Trust me, when you start reading a poorly written book, you will get frustrated in a hurry, and will probably not respect the author, even if you decide to finish the book. You will probably not read that author again. And *you* don't want your readers to put you in that basket!

Look at your manuscript so far. Check for the following:

1. Does the narrative use varied sentence structure? In other words, does it go beyond subject-verb-object sentences?

2. Find a few examples of complex sentences, or compound sentences, or even compound-complex sentences. Those are sentences that contain commas somewhere in them. But beware: a big no-no is separating the verb from the subject of a sentence with a comma. Don't do that. Longer sentences frequently reflect deeper, more detailed thoughts of a character (the writer), and can therefore move the plot along better.

3. Are there strong, specific action verbs? Jot down a few examples that really strike you.

4. Are there varied, colorful, specific adjectives? Jot down a few that really strike you.

5. If the story starts in the past tense, does the narrative *stay* in the past tense? If it starts in present tense, does it *stay* in present tense? That's pretty important for the flow of your story. Switching back and forth from present to past to present can be really tricky and you may find yourself losing your thread of thought and getting confused about who did what when. So, especially if this is your first effort, pick one tense and stick with it.

6. Or, if there are flashbacks, are you clear on where a flashback starts and where the plot comes back to the present?

7. Is the writing free of grammar mistakes and spelling mistakes? If you find some problems jot them down and offer a suggestion for correction.

Style Editing

Style editing has to do with the *how* of your writing: how it looks and reads on the page. That means that if, for example, Ernest Hemingway is your favorite author, you love his clean, clear, kind of 'no frills' prose without adjectives and adverbs and frequently simple sentence after simple sentence, and you find yourself rereading his novels every now and then just for the sheer pleasure of it, you don't want to try to write a novel in the style of TR Pearson, who writes wonderfully funny and touching novels but whose sentences can each go on for a page or two.

The best advice I can ever give writers is: write like you talk. That makes your writing come out authentic on the page, believable to anyone who picks up your book. Trying to use stilted vocabulary and sentence structure, even if you're writing about Victorian London and you want to use appropriate dialogue and sentence structure, will land you in difficulty because that's not your natural way of talking. And everyone will pick up on that sooner rather than later.

Your personal style is the form you revert to every time you write something, even a friendly letter. So your style may be clean and sparse, with few adjectives and adverbs. Or your style may be wildly imaginative – on purpose – with lots of funny descriptors that lead your readers to chuckles or laughter, or maybe funny drawings included in the body of what you write. Or somewhere in between.

Keep in mind that if you're writing a very serious novel, a very dark novel, a biography of a serious person, a memoir of some serious times, you want to check yourself that you're not writing 'flippant.' A serious subject deserves a serious style. That doesn't mean that funny things or humorous things don't happen in the midst of all that seriousness; sometimes lightening the mood occasionally can really help your readers get through the tough stuff. And a funny novel deserves some fun in its style. Use a lighter touch with vocabulary to get across the point that you yourself are having fun.

So read the manuscript through without marking on it. Just flip through. It's not necessary to read word for word. You're just trying to get a general impression. Or give your manuscript to a good friend – one who loves to read the same kinds of books you like to read – to read through.

Then think about:

- How would you improve the manuscript if it were someone else's? What things would you change? Add? Delete? Rearrange?

- Does the opening page make you want to read on? If yes, what makes it so effective?

- If it could be improved, what would you do? Improved overall – the big picture – not the smaller stuff?

- Does the manuscript writer use effective topic sentences for paragraphs? And does the topic sentence help develop the paragraph? Just scan through a few sections and check to see.

- Does the writer need more or better transitions to link paragraphs? Just check paragraphs in a few places. Quote from the manuscript where you think there is a particularly good transition. If you find a disjointed transition, or a missing transition (that makes the sequence from one paragraph to the next hard to figure out) offer a suggestion to make the transition logical.

- Does the writer (you?) use sufficient details and examples? If so, give a couple of examples where the writer has used detail effectively, quoting directly from the manuscript. If not, suggest where the writer could incorporate more details and examples.

- Are there any words, phrases or sentences that aren't clear? If so, offer the writer some suggestions.

- Do you see any problems with spelling, grammar, or punctuation? Don't fix their mistakes but indicate the problems they need to address.

- What's your overall impression of the narrative?

Story Editing

Story editing is similar to continuity editing, but looks at the overarching *plot* of the manuscript and assumes that you've already looked at individual sections or chapters to make sure they hang together internally, individually. This is kind of like the 'elevator speech' that job seekers are taught about: can you explain this plot in two or three sentences so that I know what the overall story is? You want to double check your manuscript to make sure your story makes sense all the way through. You've had the big picture discussion with yourself so now you need to make sure that picture ends as well as it began. You want to make sure there aren't any characters left hanging at the end of the story; we know what's happened to everyone in your plot for good or ill. You don't have any secondary plot lines left hanging. Even if you want to save some thunder for a sequel to this story you need to make that clear. Readers don't want to be left hanging.

You might want to do some story checking, looking for coherence after each three or four chapters and not just at the end of the story. As you read through your manuscript think about the following:

1. Can you get a general idea of what the story line is? If yes, what is it? Can you describe the plot in only two or three sentences?

2. Does it make sense?

3. Can you briefly summarize the main plot so far?

4. Do any ideas seem vague? What can you (or the writer) explain more thoroughly that would help the reader?

5. Does the introduction give the reader 'clues' about the plot and the characters?

6. As a reader, do you sense a structure in the manuscript? Can you determine a logic in the plot? Are the ideas easy to follow in their arrangement?

7. Do transitions between paragraphs and between chapters or sections help to connect ideas? If not, what could the writer do to make transitions make more sense?

8. Is the story so far interesting? What is the most interesting section of the story so far?

9. Are there some sections of the manuscript that are better written than others? Are these sections better focused, with ideas more completely defined?

10. Is the conclusion a real conclusion or just a summary? Does the conclusion refer backwards to the introduction of the story and help to round out the whole plot? You really want a conclusion and not a summary at the end of your book. The difference: a summary is merely a list of the key points you've made all the way through your book and leaves it at that. A real conclusion may list all those points, or just the major ones, but it also pulls all those plot threads together into one big spool that the reader can get a handle on and so be satisfied with how everything came together in the end. That means the reader will be more likely to pick up your next book.

Research: Tips for Re-creating What You Don't Know for Sure

You're writing an autobiography, a biography, a memoir, a historical novel.

But you've come to spots where you have no written, confirmed documentation to help you make a point.

But you are pretty sure you *know* how things went, just the same. And you want to stay out of trouble, for sure! You don't want to recreate an exact conversation that you can't prove if anyone calls you on it.

So, how do you "re-create" what you pretty well know happened or who said what, if you weren't there?

First, remember, generally for autobiographies, biographies and memoirs, that you must tell the truth as best you remember it, or perhaps as well as someone you have interviewed remembers it. The truth is always best. Be honest about what you know and don't know.

However, you are allowed to describe events that might have occurred or really did occur, but you don't know or can't remember them exactly, as long as:

- You let the reader into your head and as long as
- Those particular written sequences are absolutely in line with what you think probably really happened or
- How someone you've interviewed thinks something probably happened.

Fortunately, there are some things you can do to deconstruct the internal truths you're pretty sure you know but can't verify.

Here are some things you can do for autobiography, memoir, historical fiction:

- Go ahead and write the appropriate dialogue between characters that you've heard in your head, or you're almost sure they probably had, but you have no way of checking on it. **But** somewhere in your text say something like:

    o The dialogue has been almost entirely reconstructed from research notes

    o The dialogue is *essentially* true (and I know this because…)

    o The dialogue is *re-created* according to what my grandfather remembers

    o The characters' names have been changed or modified; but the situation really occurred

- With histories, historical fiction, autobiography, biography and memoir you can take small liberties with the time line of your story or with the chronology. **But** somewhere in your text say something like:

  o   All events actually did happen (and I know this because….)

  o   I've taken small liberties with the chronology of events in order to help the reader understand the importance of….. (situation, action, person, character)

  o   I've blurred the truth of a specific situation with a bit of fiction to protect……. (person, in particular, although you don't have to name the person, you can perhaps give a job title)

  o   I've conflated several situations/events into a smaller time frame to help the reader better understand the era/age/year…..

  o   For the purposes of my narrative I have moved the events of May 1949 to June, because I'm not absolutely sure of the exact date(s)/time(s) when they actually happened, in order to move the narrative forward and keep the tension of the story line.

- If your memory of an event is confused or has gaps you can say something like:

  o   I can't remember exactly who said this but what happened was…

  o   I can't remember who did what but I do remember that….

  o   I didn't actually say that but I do remember basically what I said and I have come close to what I actually said (or, she didn't actually say that but…)….

  o   This event was reported by my grandmother Rose and I have extrapolated parts of what she remembers

- You can decide you want to entirely omit an event or events from your narrative. That's fine. Just don't start writing about the omitted event somewhere in your narrative where it *didn't* happen. Your readers will begin to distrust you.

- A wonderful tool to use when you don't know something for sure: conditionals. These are words and phrases you can use to help recreate a situation when you weren't actually physically there:

  - I imagine
  - It could be
  - It seems that
  - Supposedly
  - Perhaps
  - Maybe
  - It's likely that
  - I suppose
  - He/she always/usually
  - It appears that
  - As a consequence of
  - As a result of
  - Despite
  - No matter how
  - Supposing that
  - It was predicted that
  - Feeling (embattled and vulnerable) … he must have appreciated…. (the kind letter)
  - It is suggested by (the number of letters sent to him) that…
  - It seemed (to him/her)
  - It appeared (to)
  - Evidently (he evidently took no action because he stayed home…)
  - It's been claimed that
  - Although undoubtedly

- Before you think you're ready to publish, ask people who are still living about what they said in years past before you publish. Get their 'reporting' of their own conversations and then compare to what you've written.

- For memoir, autobiography, or biography, don't make up situations or people or events. *Ever.*

- Show your manuscript, or read out loud appropriate parts, to anyone who is included in it who is still around, before you get to a publisher. And you might be wise to check with relatives of a deceased person too if you're not sure how they'll think about what you write.

- And for heavens' sake, don't copy someone else's piece of writing. That's called plagiarism and it can get you into BIG trouble! That means don't borrow from your great aunt Minnie's diary entries by copying them word for word, if great aunt Minnie is still around. *Unless you have explicit written permission from her.* Even if Minnie has gone to her reward, you're still better off adapting what she said or rephrasing, or rewording. Or if you do take her writing word for word, it might be wise to put sentences in quotation marks.

- And don't borrow from old newspapers or books or diaries or journals unless they are out of copyright and in the public domain. If you absolutely need a piece of writing word for word from someone else, cite it formally in your notes. If you need to depend on someone else's research be sure you cite it somewhere in your text.

- Finally, all the above should not be regarded as strictures to your own writing. In most instances you can put such disclaimers all together in the introduction to your work. You can take care of all of them at the same time, if you need to.

- Or it is becoming more and more common to put all citations at the very end of your manuscript. That means putting the citation number with the citation itself, but putting the sources all together in a section at the back of the book. The good thing about collecting them up all in one place is that you can do further explaining if you need to, so if you felt that some piece of information didn't quite fit into your narrative, you can offer further explanation in your end notes.

- So: you cite the chapter number, the page number, or even sometimes the paragraph number, and your reference. Then you might say something like: James Smith of Cambridge University says that Marie Antoinette also had frequent assignations with Count Bernadotte, but that research has never been substantiated.
- Or it might look something like: Chapter 8. 80 (citation number). Thomas, 108. (Your reference author and page number). Colwell makes the same point as Chantal Thomas in her revolutionary pamphlets describing…….

The Emotional Stuff

Tips to Help You Get Past Frustration with That Plot

OK, now let's deal with some of the emotional stuff that goes along with writing a best-seller.

You've written up a storm for days and days or weeks and weeks but all of a sudden nothing comes.

You've lost the thread of your plot.

You've decided you don't even like one or more of your characters.

Or you're just tired of the physical act of doing the writing, even if it's so easy on the computer.

If you're frustrated or overwhelmed you can try:

1. Put your manuscript aside and read a new mystery or romance or horror story or adventure story or biography or memoir. Or look at several book reviews of the type of book you're writing to see how the art of writing that particular format has changed over time. For example, in biographies or memoirs, not all plots follow one or more characters from birth to death anymore. Many of them these days just cover part of their subject's life. Get on Amazon and see what's good right now.

2. If you are writing a book that needs research, keep writing even as you keep researching. If you stop writing, or you don't even think you should start writingt till you think you've got all your researching done, you'll never get to the writing part.

3. But also, you might want to do some major time on research at the outset. Even if you encounter more than one dead end, you will still learn more and more about your subject as you go along.

4. But! Don't feel like you must include every piece of research you've ever done. That could get very boring very fast if some pieces of research don't move your story line along. You might save those bits and pieces for your next novel or your second volume of your subject's life.

5. If you're writing a biography, allow the 'story' to emerge on its own from your interviews and research. Don't get hung up on going in only the direction you thought you wanted to go in at the beginning. You might discover a whole different 'plot' than you thought you would have when you first got interested in this person.

6. Keep a file with photos, illustrations, letters, other kinds of print documents that you want to use as you write. If you want to use any of them in your text, be aware that some of them may require someone's permission to publish them. You need to find that out early on in the process. Get permissions before you send your manuscript to a publisher. That may save you work and heartache if it should happen that you can't obtain some of those permissions and you've already finished your manuscript.

7. If you're an artist you can include appropriate reproductions of your drawings or paintings or poems or photographs in your text. You can take a break from writing to hunt for or actually paint/photograph your won art work. We are such a visual society that readers usually really enjoy seeing visual references to what you're writing about.

8. Think about how your book will read five or ten or more years from now. If there's an important historical anniversary coming up, for example, your book may be a bigger hit than you even thought it would be.

9. Do not worry if someone else, or even several other people, has written a book with a similar plot or about a similar situation or about the same person you're writing a biography on. Your story will look different from everyone else's and that will stand you in good stead.

10. Include some of the real historical events going on around your character, real person or fictional, whether you're writing about a real person or you're writing a novel. Those will help your readers put your person's/characters' life into historical perspective, and provide extra interest besides. And that kind of research can be fascinating in itself to you if you're bogged down.

11. When you get bogged down, just enjoy the writing. You never know what direction your person will take you in and you may learn things you don't even know you didn't know. Maybe set a time limit - say, I'm going to write for at least 60 minutes every day (or however many minutes you can stomach) even if what I write isn't wonderful. I can always come back to it later and revise or toss out.

12. Change the time of day that you do your writing. You might find that you like a different time better.

13. Change the place where you write. Just a change of 'scenery' might do wonders. Go outside. Go sit in a park. Sit in a coffee shop. Just move.

14. Join a writing group. Or join a professional writers' organization. There are many of them out there, and sometimes you just need to vent about your writing problems or your writer's block with someone who's been there and done that!

Tips for Structuring a Writing Group

Writing groups are wonderful for helping aspiring writers with lots of things: telling you when a scene is particularly well written, or a chapter is particularly haunting, or a character is particularly compelling. As well as letting you know when you've gotten off track, or you've left some big chunk of important information out of a scene, or one chapter just doesn't make sense to the rest of the plot. If nothing else, members of a writing group have great shoulders to cry on!

If you want to set up a writing group and you can get a couple of other people together, during your first meeting:

1. Decide on what the goals are for your writing group:
    *   What does each of you want from the group? Talk it through at the very first meeting. That may save you from little problems later on in your sessions.
    *   Do you want firm deadlines for bringing in your manuscripts to discuss? In other words, do you want to perhaps rotate who brings a manuscript to each session - that means that each person has an assignment due date that stays firm.
    *   Do you want to allot time to actually do some writing in the group session?
    *   Do you want to stick with only the people in your group right now or will you be open to adding new members?

2. Decide on a format for the group sessions:
    *   How often do you want to meet?
    *   Where do you want to meet?
    *   Do you want one person to read from their work at each meeting? Or maybe everyone reads?
    *   Do you want each person to provide enough copies for each other person to have one of their own to read and critique during your meeting? Or is reading out loud from one copy enough for the group?
    *   Do you want people to send in their manuscript by e mail before the meeting and then have a discussion/critique during the meeting?
    *   Do you want someone to lead the group? Or do you want to rotate leadership? Or do you want no leader?
    *   Do you want a secretary? Do you want someone to be responsible for sending reminder emails to the rest of the group?

3. Set some ground rules:
    *   There will always be some circumstances that might cause a mix up or a mash up. So what is your back up plan for the meeting? Decide on what to do in the case that the person assigned to bring a manuscript forgets to write anything that week. Or three of you come down with the flu at the same time and need to stay home in bed, but three of you are perfectly healthy.
    *   Do you hold your group meeting regardless?
    *   Is there a writing exercise the group could do in extenuating circumstances?

- You might want to time each person's reading or talking about their own writing, to keep one person from monopolizing the group every meeting. If you find that you have one person who tends to dominate the meeting and does most of the talking without letting others speak, try the *marble jar* process. All the marble jar process requires is a number of marbles and an empty jar. Hand out an equal number of marbles to each person around the table and set the empty jar in the middle of the table. Each person must toss a marble into the jar each time he or she makes a comment. When the dominating person's marbles are all gone, she suddenly ceases to dominate the conversation! But…. Stick to your guns and you'll see how quickly the group gets democratic once again.
- What's your process going to be for responding to each writer's reading?

4. Limit the socializing:
   - Decide on a time and a space for socializing at each meeting. Maybe five or ten minutes before the end of the meeting. Or even five or ten minutes at the beginning of the meeting. You might as well schedule that kind of time in; you know you will chit chat anyway…..
   - End of the session works best because you run less of a risk in getting the group sidetracked.
   - Or try taking a break in the middle of the meeting, but be aware that someone will have to be the time keeper.
   - But note: brefreshments can work wonders for a writing group. I have encouraged them with each of my writing groups; nothing fancy and nothing complicated and nothing expensive. Just keep it simple and don't get overly dependent on refreshments or your group may get sidetracked more than you would like.

5. Set up a consistent process for offering feedback. You want to give good, constructive feedback. Just saying a piece of writing is 'good' or 'boring' doesn't help. You need to be much more specific if you want your group members to value your critique, and see you as a valued member of the group. Questions you probably want to ask, at a minimum:
   - What's working in the narrative?
   - Is the structure of the narrative hanging together?
   - What catches your attention first in the narrative?
   - Where are you fascinated and wanting to hear more?
   - What parts do you remember most?
   - What parts are slow to read? Why?
   - Did any part of the narrative confuse you? If so, where and what?
   - Is there a problem with any sentence structure? Spelling? Over-used words or phrases?
   - What's your absolute favorite part of the narrative so far?
   - And you might want to assign various members to run off paper copies of your evaluation sheet so each participant can take home the critiques to study and use.

6. So that probably means you need some kind of a formatted evaluation sheet, one that stays the same over time. Decide at an early meeting what items you want on your sheet and stick to it. The bulleted list above is fine for your evaluation sheet, so use it if you want to. Just leave enough space on the sheet for people to write or jot some notes. And make sure you use the same format every meeting. You might assign a different person to run off copies before each meeting, so everyone takes a turn.

7. Also, set up a process for *accepting* feedback. Writing is hard work, in case you haven't figured that out yet. At this point in your life, writing may be your 'real' job. And no one wants a negative job review. Your ultimate goal as a writer is to make your narrative as interesting and enlightening and enjoyable as possible. So your group wants to make everyone comfortable to accept feedback that addresses their problems as well as their successes. Just be sure each person knows that they have the right to change or not change anything brought up about their writing. I've outlined a form that's a good process for feedback but there are certainly other formats, some written and some orally delivered that you can find or design in the group.

8. Talk through early on what makes good feedback and what is not constructive. So, in other words, if feedback is negative about any place in the narrative each person can say what's not working in the manuscript but:
   - Stick to the written word, not the writer's personality
   - Be very specific
   - Give concrete examples of what's not working: page numbers, paragraph numbers
   - Be careful: writing is not bad or good innately (unless it's so full of typos or bad grammar or poor spelling); any particular plot works for some of us but not for others, so you're not telling any group member that their writing is bad. Tell them what's not working, not that they are a bad writer.
   - You might limit negative comments to only one or two at a time, if you're really having a rough go with someone's writing. Give them time to work on one or two things to correct; that's about what a person can handle in a day.
   - After all, you want people to keep coming back……

9. And, thinking outside the box: what about group field trips?
   - To author readings: book stores are usually really good at offering author readings and signings.
   - Or check out library events.
   - Or check out local store bulletin boards for writing events.
   - Or check out what writing conferences are close to you that you all might enjoy.
   - Or check out local scenes of interest that might lend themselves to some creative writing, even if you're not writing a novel. You never know what you might come back to somewhere in your own writing that turns out to be useful.

Take a Break: At the Movies

Take a break from the serious stuff!

Here's something that might get you past a moment of frustration. Make yourself feel really good about your novel, your biography, you memoir! And, yes, movies get made of all three kinds of plots. Just think about how successful *Patton* was, or *The Blind Side* or *Lawrence of Arabia*, or *Joy* just to name a few.

Your book's movie rights have just been sold to Steven Spielberg for a humongous sum of money.

1. Who has Spielberg signed to be the lead roles? Two supporting roles?

2. The hard part: the movie will only make zillions of dollars if he can cut the screen play to under two and a half hours. And of course there won't be any Oscars for the movie unless you can cut some out of the middle. Which three scenes from the middle of your manuscript would you cut? Why?

Writers Evaluation Sheet

Read the manuscript in front of you but do not mark on it.

After you've read through it, or when time is called jot some notes on:

Three places that really work:

1.

2.

3.

Three places that don't work:

1.

2.

3.

Three things to work on:

1.

2.

3.

The Art (and Work) of Getting Published

Do You Need a Professional Editor?

After you've done all you could editing your manuscript yourself and after your good friends and neighbors have critiqued it the best they can and after you've spell-checked it to death… you decide that you'd really like an impartial observer to read it, someone who knows how to make your manuscript read smoothly and sharply and look good and, mostly, to tell you what you've missed and what could be made better.

- So you decide to try to find a professional editor. A professional editor can punch up your manuscript to make agents and publishing companies want very badly to represent you. A book doctor (editor) can work with you on your story line in several ways.

- There are basically four facets to a professional edit:
    - A *continuity edit* makes sure you don't get your plot confused.
    - A *word choice edit* works at the word level.
    - A *developmental edit* helps you back up and think about various parts of your plot.
    - A *story edit* looks at the big picture.

- Costs for editing can go several ways:
    - Surface level edit – the story edit - of your manuscript will probably run you $30.00 to $60.00 an hour.

    - The continuity and/or developmental edit goes a little deeper into your manuscript to point out problems and will probably run you $35.00 to $75.00 an hour.

    - If you want the whole nine yards, including the word and sentence and line editing, that involves a much closer reading of your manuscript and will cost between $50.00 and $80.00 an hour.

    - E book editing is usually about $50.00 an hour.

    - Most of the time people will quote you a price, and you might want to shop around.

    - Professional editors will offer you a contract that lays out what you can expect and what you can reasonably expect them to do.

    - You should choose how specific you want an editor to get: do you want to go down to the word level, or are you pretty happy at that level but you just want to make sure you've got a dynamite, connected, can't put it down book.

    - Some editors will offer a contract that depends on the number of *hours* they spend on your manuscript rather than the different types of editing they will do. Or they prefer to charge by the word or by the page. If you're on a limited budget and/or you're already feeling pretty good about your finished product, this might be the option for you because you're the one in control here.

- Whichever option you choose, READ THE CONTRACT! And then READ THE CONTRACT again! And make sure you *get* a contract before turning your manuscript over to someone else.

- Because: The bad thing is that they can hold you hostage when they keep sending you back your manuscript for revisions – at a cost each time

So before you bring in a professional there are a few things you can do to help you decide if you really need a professional:

- Go back and reread one more time. Every time you come to an overused cliché cut it and all the words surrounding it! It might be hard to cut out your jewels but it works!

- Check for sections that got off-topic. You may find that you have a whole chapter (let's hope not more than one) that kind of wanders into territory you don't even want to go into. Cut it!

- Check your descriptions of people, places and things. You might discover that you have spent three pages on the description of a minor character and now you're wondering why. Cut it! Or you've spent four paragraphs describing the hotel bathroom or the restaurant furnishings and now you're wondering why you need that much description of a scene that only appears once. Cut it!

- If you look at a passage that you're not sure about, think hard about it. Can you justify that much verbiage in that particular space? Does it really make sense there? Is it really moving your story line along? If you can't think of a reason – now, really think – cut it! Readers generally want to see really tight writing that reflects really tight plot lines. They don't want lots of wandering around as you try to get from one plot point to the next one.

- One caveat: don't just toss the words, phrases, sentences and paragraphs; hang on to them. File them away for future use. You never know when your jewels might find a better home somewhere else in your writing.

If you've done these five things and you really like what you're reading now, you may not even want a professional. You might be well on your way to the next step, which is finding an agent, or getting your manuscript ready for self-publishing.

However, you might still want to get a professional editor if:

- You've contacted an agent and the agent tells you she really likes your story but it needs some real editing to make it sellable to a publisher.

- Or the agent may really like what you have but doesn't even want to submit it to a publisher till you've made some substantial changes to make it tighter.

- You've gotten to a publisher who really likes what you've got but wants some major changes.

- You want to self-publish but you want to make sure you don't have lots of typos and spellos that you are afraid you've missed and you want your manuscript to look as professional as possible.

So where do you go to find a professional editor? I must tell you it's not easy unless you live in New York City or Los Angeles or Boston. Their names just don't appear in your local yellow pages. However, there are some places you can check out to see if you can find an editor that suits you and your pocketbook.

- Go online and look up 'professional editor' or 'book doctor.'

- If you have a college or a college branch near you gather up your courage and call the English Department to see if they can recommend someone to you.

- A few web sites: the Editorial Freelancers' Association – www.the-efa.org or the Professional Editors Network – www.pensite.org or www.elance.org. Scroll through and look for editors that might suit you.

- Look at the end pages or the dedication page or the acknowledgements page of your favorite authors. Do they thank their editors? Many best-selling authors do thank their editors for all their help because they realize how much the editor has improved their manuscript. If your favorite authors list their editors by name, take a bit of time and see if those editors have web pages or e mail addresses. Check out their sites to see if you find one you really like the sound of. You might want to gather up your courage and contact one of them. Just be aware that if the editor is successful enough to be acknowledged by a best-selling author, you will be paying more toward the higher end of the dollar scale for their services. But you never know: you could send them a few pages of your manuscript – ones that you feel are most compelling – and they may decide to at least look over your stuff. If so, you're on your way. If not, nobody's going to steal your stuff, because they don't know your whole plot.

After all these leads, if you're still stuck, look around at your friends. You probably have at least one who likes to write and whom you know is a good writer. Why don't you try asking that friend to be your editor? Between the two of you draft a contract using the information you've got about what editors do, and sign and go! There may be ups and downs in this relationship, but there would be ups and downs between you and a professional as well. An advantage of hiring a friend is that she may be much more accessible to you than a professional, who is probably juggling several manuscripts at the same time.

And, lastly, if you find a professional editor you think you're going to like, check references. By that I mean: if you've found an editor's name in one of your favorite author's books you know what kind of editing he does, so that part's solved. If you go to a web site to find a professional editor, before you sign a contract do some reading of what he's edited in his professional life: it might be published books, or it might be theses or dissertations or scientific research or volumes of poetry. Whatever types of manuscript this editor has handled you need to make a decision if his editing style matches with your writing style. If he's a fit, head for the contract.

Agents

Now that you're happy – at last! – with your manuscript it's time to start thinking about the next steps to getting published. So a logical next step is to search out a professional agent. Before you get that far here are some things you might want to know about what agents can and can't do. This is not an easy or a quickly automatic process. All you have to do is think about JK Rowling, who submitted her first Harry Potter manuscript to something like fifteen agents and companies before someone finally believed in her. So have patience with this step.

Generally speaking, if you want to get published by an international publisher: get an agent. So here's the down and dirty.

- Agents are the gatekeepers. If you want to submit your manuscript to a national reputable publisher, you probably won't get to a reputable publisher's desk without first going through an agent.

- The first thing to know is that, if at all possible, you need an agent who deals with the type of writing you do. That means your agent will 'get' what you write, will understand where your plot is coming from. Someone who likes to read what you like to read. And that means someone who will have a vested interest in getting your manuscript to a publisher. So if you've written a mystery, for example, search around for an agent who frequently handles mysteries.

- 99% of the time you can't get a book anywhere without an agent.

- Be aware: an agent's job is <u>not</u> to edit and rewrite your book.

- An agent should sign a contract with you and go out and get you a book deal.

- Agents should not cost you anything! They usually get 15% of the profit if they sell the book. If they don't sell the book they don't get paid. Their job is to get your book very quickly into the hands of someone at a reputable publishing company who has decision-making capability. However, do note that you may be the one paying for copying or shipping or some other minor costs.

- Agents generally work with a publisher (but they are on your side) to get you the best contract possible, the best earning possibilities in ways you might not even have imagined.

- A good agent can also help you with additional possibilities to earn you dollars, like TV rights or movie rights.

- The publisher pays all stuff, and by 'stuff' I mean the publishing costs, the cover art for the book, the promotional tours, the TV appearances, that kind of thing.

- Most contracts are set up so the publisher sends checks to your agent and then the agent sends your share on to you. A note: if you are lucky enough to get an agent and a publisher, require two checks: one to you and one to your agent.

- How do you get an agent? Unfortunately, unless you live in New York or Los Angeles, finding an agent may not be easy. If you check your local yellow pages you are not very likely to find any names. But there are some places you can look.

- For example: check www.querytracker.net for information about finding an agent:
    - You can look up agents
    - You can track your submissions

- Another good database for finding an agent is www.agentquery.com

- A great place to find names of agents is to look at the dedication pages of novels, or whatever kind of writing you do, of the authors you most enjoy and see who their agents are! Then look them up…..

- You will need to send a 'query letter' to your potential agent. But be aware that these days many agents don't respond to you if their answer is 'no.' You'll find some information about query letters in the next section.

- If you're looking for an agent don't self-publish at the same time.

- Agents want to sign you for more than one book. It's like a marriage. If your book is really good they will see future dollar signs for you both, as well as present dollar signs.

- Now on the down side, be willing to walk away from an agent if you stop seeing the long term benefits.

- Agents typically get 6 months to 1 year to sell your book before you fire them.

- Before your sign a contract you can make small demands; e.g. 'don't change my plot, don't change the gender of my characters.'

- If you can find one attend a writers' conference – there are a number of them during the year and they might be expensive to register for but there are usually agents there.

- Your agent tells you who he's sent your book to, who's been assigned to you as editor, what's your time frame to possible publishing date, etc.

- Don't give your agent total control for negotiating your contract for you; you stay up with it yourself. Pay attention at each step of the negotiations or you might end up with a deal you don't like, one that doesn't serve you well.

- Most advances are about $5000.00 but remember the 15% for your agent, and taxes. The advance comes in thirds, too, usually.

- Advances in literary fiction tend to be higher than those for genre fiction, like romances or horror stories or mysteries.

- Where else can you find agents' names?
    - The Writer's Digest annual <u>Guide to Literary Agents</u>
    - Chuck Sambuchino's *Guide to Literary Agents* blog
    - Jeff Herman's annual <u>Guide to Book Publishers, Editors, and Literary Agents</u>
    - "Agent Query": a free-to use website – <u>www.agentquery.com</u>
    - "Publisher's Marketplace": <u>www.publishersmarketplace</u>
    - *Publisher's Weekly*
    - Association of Authors' Representatives : <u>www.aaronline.org</u>
    - "Media Bistro": <u>www.mediabistro.com</u>

Questions you might ask to see if an agent is a good fit for you:

- What do you like most about my book?

- What kind of sales do you really think my book will generate?

- How will you market my book to a publisher?

- How do you want me to communicate with you? And how often?

- What's the percentage you will charge b as commission? Do you charge any other fees to anyone? If so, what are they? (Like faxing, photocopying, shipping, etc.)

- What's your experience in representing the kind of book I've written? How many have you sold?

- How many other people have you represented? How many other people have you *sold* books for?

- What happens if my book doesn't sell?

- How do you handle royalties and advances?

Four things that let you know you need a new agent:

- Your agent ends up not selling your manuscript

- Your agent doesn't respond to your phone calls or e mails.

- Your agent seems less than fascinated by your work

- Your agent tries to pass you off to some other agent

Query Letters

You can send a query letter to a publisher as well as to an agent. However, remember what I've said about agents being the gatekeepers for the major publishers. Sending a publisher an unsolicited manuscript will probably not get you very far. And sending an unsolicited manuscript to an agent without first seeing if the agent will accept your manuscript may be frustrating and fruitless as well. So go with a query letter to an agent first if you want to go the national publisher route.

- If you decide to send a 'query letter' to your potential agent, and perhaps to your publisher of choice, be aware that these days many agents don't respond to you if their answer is 'no.' And it isn't wise to query an agent and a publisher at the same time. Agents like to have your manuscript first to work with since they have more inside knowledge of publishers.

- Make your query 1 page only. Use description to explain your plot, typically similar language to the blurb that would be on the back of the book. A good rule of thumb is to stick to a couple of hundred words only in your letter.

- What does a query letter look like and how do you write one? The site www.queryshark.com is a good site for learning how to write a good query.

- A couple of places you might look to help with query letters: The Writer's Guide to Query Letters by Wendy Burt-Thomas; or How to Write Irresistible Query Letters by Lisa Collier Cool.

- When you write your query letter, either to an agent or to a publisher, be sure to stick within published guidelines if there are any. In other words, if the manuscript submission form calls for 100 words, don't even have 101!

- Don't include two manuscripts at one time and only describe one manuscript in your query letter.

- If an agent responds positively to your query letter you need to make sure your book is already almost finished. Because if they like your query letter they'll ask for a 'partial,' which is typically three chapters.

- Be patient – it may take a long time for an agent to reply and get everything in the works.

- And you can certainly send a query letter to more than one agent at a time. There's nothing unethical about that. Actually, if you've found several agents that you like, it might help you speed up the process if you query them all!

- You can also – if you're brave enough - get an agent on the phone and do a quick query right out loud and then offer to follow up with a letter and the manuscript. But then get the letter in the mail right away before the agent forgets who you are.

- If you get lucky enough to find an agent anywhere near you, say within driving distance, offer to meet the agent at their convenience and buy them a cup of coffee. Make your pitch out loud, but a good idea is to have your formal query letter with you so that you can hand it over immediately.

- Four things you need to include in your query letter at the very least:
    - What's your book about in the first place?

    - Why would anyone want to read it?

    - What made you write the book? This is kind of the "Who died and made you King" question. Why you and not someone else? What's your writing or research biography (background)? What qualifies you to write this book?

    - Why have you chosen this particular agent? A little gentle flattery might get you anywhere, but tell the truth. Remember to choose an agent or publisher who knows your type of book and then tell why you chose this agent and not someone else.

- But also remember the one-page rule. So be concise.

- That being said, you might want to attach part of a chapter of your book or maybe even a whole chapter. But pick a really strong section. And don't worry that anyone will steal your glorious prose. After all, no one else knows where you're going with your plot.

What to avoid when you're trying to find/work with an agent:

- Gimmicks: you don't want to make jokes or mail funny or odd things to an agent or otherwise make him nervous about you.

- Don't send your manuscript and/or letter packages wrapped so it's impossible to open!

- Don't use teeny tiny fonts or huge fonts that make a manuscript look a whole lot longer than it really is.

- Don't use weird or funky fonts. Check the publisher's requirement about font type and size.

- Misspelling the agent's name or the publishing company's name is a huge no-no…

- Trying to get the agent to take on more than one of your manuscripts at one time (you should be so lucky as to have two at one time, right?) is self-defeating; your agent can only handle one manuscript at a time fully.

- Not putting your return address on your manuscript or using a post office box should be a 'duh' so pay attention.

- And for heaven's sake make sure the grammar, the punctuation, and the sentence structure in your letter are all correct. This is not the time for cutesy prose.

The Book Proposal

Let's talk about nonfiction for a bit. Most nonfiction books are placed with a reputable publisher on the basis of a book proposal. A book proposal is much more extensive than a query letter. If you have an idea for a good autobiography, biography, memoir, or history, you may be tempted to go directly to a publisher and skip the agent process.

But you can send your book proposal to your agent, if you've contracted with one, and he will send it on if it looks promising.

Whereas novels are completely finished before they are submitted to an agent or a publisher you don't have to be finished with your nonfiction effort in order to submit a book proposal.

Book proposals may be for a book that isn't finished yet or is still in outline form. In particular, if you have a scholarly work, you might want to submit a book proposal to a university press or other publishing company known for publishing research

A book proposal to a publisher is very much like a cold call that someone trying to sell you something on the phone might make, so you really need to take your courage in hand if you want to go this route. So your book proposal needs to be very well-crafted, "bullet proof."

But if this is your preference, after you've researched some publishers that you like the sound of:

- A book proposal is a detailed description of what your book is about. You need to have at least a couple of good chapters already written to include in your proposal.

- You need to have a completed outline of your whole plot, or an outline for at least as far as it is completed so far.

- You need to tell the publisher why he wants to publish your book on _____ subject rather than someone else's book on the same subject. You need to tell the publisher how your book is different from anyone else's on the same subject.

- You need to tell the publisher where there is a hole in the particular market around your subject, a hole that justifies your book.

- You need to need to show that you've done your homework on your subject – through the materials you include in your packet.

- You need to talk about who is going to read this book: who is the audience?

- And it's a good idea if you write a little about what you want readers of this book to take away from it when they have finished reading it.

A good book proposal should convince a publisher that your book is good enough to stand beside others on the same subject, but yours approaches the subject from a different enough point of view that it really needs to go on that bookshelf.

So, you might organize your proposal with:

1. A summary of your book in a couple of paragraphs.

2. A brief biography of yourself and what skills, knowledge, degrees qualify you to write this particular book.

3. The competition: who else has written a book about this same subject – brief list – and why your book is better or fits right in with other similar books.

4. A completed outline of your book.

5. Two or three completed chapters, preferably consecutive chapters, so the publisher can get a sense of the continuity of your 'story'. It helps is you have *the first three* chapters completed.

6. A timeline of when you think your manuscript will be completed, and what's your approximate word count.

7. An annotated table of contents

A book proposal, unlike the query letter which you try to keep as succinct as possible, is usually between 25 and 50 pages long, *not counting* the chapters you include in the packet. So this takes some time and organizing and effort on your part.

And last, but certainly not least, put a good cover letter at the top of your proposal. Your cover letter will contain numbers 1, 2, and 3 above in much abbreviated form. One page is the best, but two will usually fly.

Researching Publishers

Large reputable publishers are still mostly located in New York City. However, in this day of enhanced technology, when publishers can print from a Word document or an html. document, or a docx. document, there are increasing numbers of good legitimate publishers in places outside New York City. And now you can communicate through e mail and Skype so you don't necessarily have to trudge to the company's home every time you need to communicate with them. If you decide you want to submit your manuscript directly to a reputable publisher you probably ought to do some research into the various publishing houses that are still around and in good standing with writers.

As you begin to search for a publisher remember something I said earlier: look for publishers who routinely publish the kind of book you write. Novel, memoir, biography, history, autobiography, or even a technical manual. Those publishers will be much more willing to accept your manuscript if they think it fits their business model. You may have suspected this already but publishers are in the business to make money, not necessarily to publish the next literary classic. So if you can match your manuscript subject to their preferences you have a leg up!

So, how do you go about finding a compatible publisher?

1. Go into a bookstore and browse through the section with books you tend to read most often and check to see which publishers are most represented. Frequently, publishing company names are right there on the spine of the book. Alternatively, they are likely found right inside the front cover. List them and look them up.

    a. Look at the book jackets of some of the books. Are they professionally done? Can you see your book with one of their covers?
    b. Is the paper the book is printed on the good stuff or really thin and kind of sallow looking?
    c. If there are photographs, drawings or other reproductions of other artwork do they look clear and colorful (if appropriate) or are they grainy or too dark or too light?
    d. How about the font size and type, and the way the text is set on the page?
    e. How about margins of the text: standardized or all over the place?
    f. Overall, does this publisher put out a book that feels really good in your hands? Readers know exactly what I mean, how it feels to get a really quality book into your hands and to love it from the first pages.

2. Look through your own home library to see which publishing companies are represented among your books. Look them up.

3. Go into your local library branch and look through the bookshelves for publishers' names.

4. Get on line and look up a term like "book publishers." Go to the web sites of the ones that sound good to you and see what they say about themselves. Remember that very often nowadays companies publish their requirements and deadlines online only and not inside any books or manuals.

5. If you get on the publisher's web site go all the way through it. Don't just look at the pictures and the 'sound bytes' you find on the first few pages.

   a. So: be sure you read the "About Us" or "About _____Publishing Company" pages. Those pages should clearly state the company's mission, and you can decide if your mission and theirs are a good match.
   b. Also look to see which current authors they represent. See anybody you know? Is this a company where you'd like to have your own name listed in the author section?
   c. Look at a few of the titles the publisher is representing. Can you tell if they are doing a really conscientious job of publicizing their authors? Do they list what awards their authors are receiving? Can you tell if their authors are getting what you consider good media coverage? That may not seem extremely important to you at this point, but think down the road; isn't that something you want for your book?

6. You can use a site I've mentioned before: www.querytracker.net to find publishers.

7. Another site you can use is www.publishersmarketplace.com .

8. If you should be lucky enough to have a friend who has successfully published a book, pick her brain for how she went about choosing a publisher and her experience with that publisher.

9. Check out some of the blogs writers post about their publishing company. Their experiences are probably different from what yours would be, but you never know….

When you think you've researched enough go back through any notes you've taken and make sure you're going with a company where you really will get the best treatment and the best deal for your kind of book. Think about this: if you get signed by a particular company you've got them until your book hits bookstores, and probably a bit after that if there's publicity to be done. Whatever you've discovered about the people who deal with you, it's not going to get any better as you go along in the publishing process. So make sure you really feel comfortable with the company you think you like best.

Check very carefully the publisher's timeline for actually shepherding a manuscript from reception to publication. In real life it will probably take a year or more to get your book onto bookshelves – remember, there are many authors with this company besides you, and the company will do their best to get your book out in a timely fashion, but it *will* take a while. And remember that your book will require some in house editing, maybe more than one pass, and that all takes time. And remember that you get the services of cover artists and layout professionals and publicity people, among others, and all of that takes some serious coordination, and time.

One caveat I would offer: if you have read at least one book by the publisher you are looking at and it is full of typos and spellos and misprints think very hard before you choose that publisher. After all, there are a whole lot more people out there besides me who will toss a book before finishing it if it's poorly edited and makes for aggravating reading.

You might also check to see how much control you'll have over the works as your book goes through the process. Double check on what input you can or cannot have into the cover of the book, the fonts, the text set up, any illustrations you want to have included in the text, the marketing of your book. That may be hard to do until you get into contract negotiations, but keep it in the back of your mind. Be aware that, as in many businesses, what you're promised and what you end up getting are not always the same.

You might also want to pay attention to the publisher's description of royalties: how much, what percentage, how often are they paid, how does the whole royalty process work within this particular company?

Most writers will get less than 10% net royalties on any book. That means that the amount you get is paid to you *after* any discounts the publisher offers to book stores for carrying your book, publicity dollars, or maybe even part of printing costs. So you'll not get rich from one book unless you really have the next best thing!

Most publishing company contracts have a 'reserve clause' in them: in other words, the company holds onto some of your royalties just in case your book gets into the bookstores but then doesn't sell well and many copies get returned to the company's warehouse.

On the up side, nowadays most contracts have an 'escalator clause' which means that if your book reaches a certain number of sales your royalty percentage goes up.

If you want to be a published writer, and you want to go with a publishing company, you really need to do your research before you select the company. May writers think they are too artsy to keep up with the financial piece of their writerly pie. They have no clue how much they are really making from their writing efforts. So some writers may not realize that they could be doing much better both artistically and financially at a different publishing company. The moral of that story is: keep up with your publishing dollars.

What to Know Before You Actually Get Published

There are some dos and don'ts to take into consideration if you want to submit your manuscript to a large publishing firm. You will want to pay attention to the written and unwritten rules for submitting manuscripts to a publisher. And, trust me, you really need to pay attention to their requirements or your manuscript will never see the light of day with that publisher.

So:

- For short stories, nonfiction articles, and poetry, only apply to trade magazines, or publishers that publish that kind of book, if you go in that direction, in fields where you have some expertise. So if you write true life hunting stories or true life fishing stories, or how-to stories, or riffs on some fad of the day, or poetry or short biographies, or little comedies, do some research and find out which companies specialize in which types of manuscripts, magazines or publishers. That is so much easier these days. All you have to do is look them up on the Internet.

- Most magazines and publishing companies only publish their publishing guidelines on their websites, not in their magazines.

- Everybody who is anybody lists their information on www.duotrope.com. It's inexpensive: you have a subscription per month
    - They list 4600 markets for poetry, short stories and short articles.
    - It's a place you can also track when and where you've already submitted stuff
    - They don't submit manuscripts themselves but you can find and track many kinds of publications and your own submissions.

- You typically get paid by the word by magazines: 3-5 cents a word for short stories and 30 cents a word for nonfiction.

- The publisher gets a one year exclusive contract with you that starts as soon as you are published. They get the publication rights. When the rights revert to you, you might want to self-publish it, and then sell it to a publisher again. But don't self-publish if you've submitted to a publisher. That's not good business practice.

- "Scrivener", www.WritersStore.com/Scrivener is a web site that provides an outlining tool; it uses cards that look like 3x5 cards. Costs about $40.00 to buy and is worth its weight in gold for those of you who like working in a Word document but want some of the convenience and comfort of working with paper organizers. It offers virtual index cards that store a synopsis for every document you create. You can also storyboard and rearrange parts of you manuscript by moving cards around on the virtual corkboard. An outliner helps you take control of the structure of your work. You can use the outliner to plan first and outline later, or write first and use the outliner to make sense of a messy first draft.

- Think about short stories too. Short fiction can help you develop a full novel because the short story is cheap to the publishers and if they like you they'll buy the whole novel when it's finished. You can place short stories in magazines of all kinds and then go from one story to the next. Short fiction will help you get from novel #1 to novel # 2 without people forgetting who you are.

- If you have written a movie script or a play script, with Scrivener you can also switch to 'scriptwriting mode' for automatic screen or stage play formatting, or set up your own script formats, then export to a dedicated scriptwriting program such as www.finaldraft.com which is a site that will help you format your manuscript to meet screenwriting guidelines. You can also mix up script formatting with regular text for writing treatments. The "snapshot of a document" function allows you to edit and rewrite, knowing you can restore an earlier version at any time.

- Long fiction: think about what you have written before you decide where to submit it. Follow the same research process as I mentioned at the beginning of this section.

- Most trade publishers will only take certain word counts. Look on their web sites to find out what their acceptable word counts are. And stick to the word count religiously! Too many words or too few most likely will get your manuscript automatically tossed…..unfortunately.

- FYI: trade books are those aimed at a specific audience. They not only contain books like engineering manuals or gardening how-to's or quilting encyclopedias but also novels like romances – those romances that are mainly published in paperback, and not hardback. Trade magazines are the same kind of thing, so be aware that *Southern Living Magazine* or *Sports Illustrated* or *Martha Stewart Living* or *Popular Mechanics* are all considered trade publications.

- Just FYI: "Novelette" = too long for a short story but too short for a novel. And a lot of publishing companies don't feel too great about taking them on, so self-publishing might really be your chance here.

- SFWA – Science Fiction Writers of America – www.sfwa.org is a major science fiction group. You might check out their web site if you're a science fiction writer.

- If you are a science fiction or fantasy writer you might check out www.writeaboutdragons.com which is a clearing house for that specific kind of plot.

- If romance writing is your thing, check out Romance Writers of America: www.rwa.org You might want to join if you want to be published. It's the most business oriented of all the writers' groups

- Any novel that has any romance at all is considered a "romance".

  - But the good news is romance readers buy any kind of fiction whereas science fiction readers usually only buy science fiction and adventure readers only buy adventure stories and thriller readers buy only thrillers.

- Romances are rated on 'heat.' To us these days that – bluntly speaking – means sex, for good or ill.
- But romances combine well with other types of genres, so you could have a 'romantic thriller,' a 'romantic mystery,' or an adventure that contains a romance as a major part of its plot. Look no farther than *Game of Thrones…..*

A Few Words about Galleys

Most often when a publishing company accepts your manuscript for publication you will eventually receive your book in 'galley' format. A galley is a copy of your book that is unbound, or sometimes in a spiral bound copy. Galley proofs are the preliminary versions of publications meant for review by authors, editors, and proofreaders, often with extra-wide margins. They aren't meant to be published as is, but to be looked over, proof read and edited by professionals at the publishing company, or professionals that are contracted by the company.

Galley proofs may be uncut and unbound. Uncut means that the paper the galley is on may be a different size than the final version will end up, and it might not be in the same format as you submitted it. In other words it may not be divided into the same sections or chapters you started out with. And if you've put illustrations or photos into your manuscript they may not be included in the galley sent to reviewers; or they may appear in black and white only. So you may literally get a box of loose pages with notations on them, with not even a paper clip on them, and full of notations about what needs to be corrected, or rearranged or revised.

Do not fear! And do not get upset. Galleys are created for proofing and editing purposes, not really to be published in front of everybody. Just know that they may be used by the company for promotional and review purposes also.

Some publishers use paper galley proofs as "advance copies," providing them to reviewers, magazines, and libraries in advance of final publication These galleys may be used to give reviewers the opportunity to provide feedback to the publisher and the writer.

"Galley proofs" are galleys issued in the intermediate stages of the publishing process. In these stages, and there will probably be more than one stage, the writer can make changes to the manuscript: text changes, chapter division changes, illustration changes, citation changes. The writer and the editor can check even the minutiae of spelling and grammar and punctuation.

And you, the writer, have the golden opportunity to tighten up your whole manuscript if it needs to be tightened. The reason there may be a number of galley stages is so that the writer and the editor can catch, hopefully, all possible mistakes in the manuscript before it goes to publication. So the writer can go through the manuscript multiple times if necessary.

"Page proofs" are proofs created in the near-final version of the manuscript, for editing and checking purposes. In the page-proof stage, mistakes are supposed to have been already corrected; for the publisher to correct a mistake at this stage is expensive, and authors are discouraged from making many changes to page proofs. Page layouts are examined closely in the page proof stage.

Page proofs also have the final pagination, any illustrations or photographs in color and in their original format and in the right places, any footnotes or end notes in their correct form, a table of contents, If included, and index, if needed, and any other extraneous things like dedications.

Nowadays, as paper and digital forms frequently become the final product that readers actually use, the term "uncorrected proof" is becoming more common as a term than galley proof, which refers exclusively to a paper proof version. "Uncorrected proof" describes the penultimate proof version (on paper or in digital form) yet to receive final author and publisher approval, the term appearing on the covers of advance reading copies

The key point to take away from receiving galleys from a publisher is not to get your nose out of joint if an editor has included many notes that tell you something fairly major needs to be done to your manuscript. That won't likely happen, but the publishing company editor who is assigned to you is acting in your best interest and is telling you what to change for your own good, so to speak. So, ,be thrilled you've gotten to the galley stage! And pay attention to what changes are suggested in the galleys and remember, you do have final approval on how your manuscript goes out into the world.

Small Presses

A small press might be your answer if you've tried the agent route to a large publishing company and haven't had any luck. Small presses are usually more amenable to taking unsolicited manuscripts than the big companies are. So you might have an easier time of getting published if you have an unusual topic, which usually means a niche topic. In other words, your subject might not appeal to the mass market, but some folks would really enjoy it or learn from it. So there's surely a reason to get your manuscript published...somewhere.

So why might you look at a small press?

- If you look at small presses, do your research: what level of support will you get? Small presses are usually relatively local; there are small presses situated throughout the country. You can find dozens of web sites for small presses, or clearing houses for small presses.

- Small presses are more likely to accept your manuscript even if you don't have an agent and haven't used a professional editor.

- Small presses are good for publishing manuscripts that have unusual topics or formats, what appeals to a more limited audience than a large market. So: poetry; birding; left-handed golf tips; caving; beach photography; neighborhood recipes. Subjects that fascinate some but not a lot of people. But there is a market out there.

- As a matter of fact, some small presses focus on only one subject so if you do a little research a small press might be just up your alley for your very targeted manuscript.

- Small religious presses might be interested in your book if it has a religious or spiritual theme. Or if you've done some research that no one else, or few others, has done and you think it should be out there.

- If you go the small press route be aware that you probably won't get an editor assigned to you, or someone to do the artwork for your cover, or a cover designer, for that matter, so you need your manuscript to be pretty pristine, unless you want problems to show up in the published book. And you don't want a sloppy looking book; people won't buy your second one if they get too aggravated with the spelling mistakes and typos and bad grammar and sloppy paragraphing. So you'll need to do your own homework first.

- And that might mean your own legwork – getting your manuscript to the company physically and going back and forth to supervise the publishing process. Which might mean you're on your e mail a lot, and consistently, since many presses now require submissions electronically. That also means you'll be responsible for any artwork or photographs or tables or charts or whatever else you want to include in your published work. So you'll need to make sure they are in the right places already when you get the manuscript to the press.

- Self-publishing also means you need to be able to be your own marketer and salesperson, since those positions don't come with that territory. So you'll need to be very self-directed in getting around to book stores – mostly small independent book stores - to get your published work onto their radar and onto their shelves.

- A university press might be considered a small press. They usually publish works by their own people but are sometimes open to publishing books by those outside their circle. However, they usually publish scholarly works and those that have required some substantive research that can be verified. If you've done some heavy-duty research on an important subject (even if you think it's only important to you), you never know, so try a university press.

- A good website for finding small presses is: www.pw.org/small_presses . It's a database of many small presses and what types of manuscripts they tend to accept.

- ***One big caveat: unless you've written a tome on something no one has ever heard of or no one else would be interested in because it's already been covered way too much, but you still feel the need to become a published author, or you have dollars and dollars to spend, be careful of what are called 'vanity presses.' A vanity press will publish anything you want to submit to them, *for a fee.* That means *you* **pay** *them* to publish your manuscript. If you have faith in your own writing ability and you think you've got a really good, a wonderful, an outstanding manuscript on your hands, why would you want to *pay* someone to publish it???? It's supposed to work the other way……

The Independent Publishing Route

If you're confident in your editing and proof reading skills and you think you've brought your manuscript to a very good conclusion, you might want to go the self-publishing route. Below is some information that might help you make that decision. Both the pros and the cons.

- Electronic printing of hard cover books and e books is becoming more and more popular with writers who have no fear of the unknown. You should know, though, that if you pursue this option you are on your own for most of the physical process of getting the book out there in the world. So you don't have an agent, an editor, a nationally known publisher, a manager, a publicist, a cover artist assigned to you.

- So if you're the shy and retiring type who can't picture yourself on the road to conferences or doing a Facebook page or creating and managing a web site, or just beating the bushes for buyers, this process is *not* for you.

- One big advantage to printing a book online or an e book is that you get 25% of an $8.00 e book, for example. That could be a lot more than you get for the first printing of a book with a publishing house.

- In self-publishing you might pay for some services you wouldn't pay for if you have a publisher: cover artist, editor, editor, proof reader…..

- Self-publishing: 1st printing is typically done on an offset press. That means that the printers print a copy of your book for a buyer on demand so they don't have to keep large numbers on hand. It's an inexpensive process for them, since they aren't responsible for keeping thousands of paper copies on hand, so that translates into higher royalties for you.

- The writer retains all rights with self-publishing, unlike a publishing company, so you retain the copyright and you 'license' the book to the self-publisher.

- Cover artists can get anywhere from $50.00 to $300.00 per cover. Professional e book artists are generally really good. You can contact cover artists by simply looking up 'cover artists' on the web and contacting one whose work you like. You can give a cover artist links to book covers you like on the web. Also give them two paragraphs of description (probably the same description for the back book cover) so they can get an idea of your plot.

- There are several web sites that will help you format your manuscript and get it ready for e book publishing, and/or paper publishing. "Create Space" – www.createspace.com , is one of the good web sites to learn how to format a book online. With this site, and with other similar sites, you can get hard copies of your book as well as submitting it for e book publishing. So, for example:

    - You can upload your book from Create Space to Amazon for free. For a fee of $25.00 they'll put it on other places.
    - Create Space doesn't' print or publish e books itself but it formats your book so Amazon will take it. They will give it an ISBN # for free, which is shared with Amazon.

- The site works you through everything from uploading and giving you the option of proofreading your manuscript to choosing cover art from their catalogue if you want it to, giving you space to write your back-of-book blurb to choosing a color scheme for the whole nine yards.
- You can order copies of your book right from the site, for a small fee, if you want some to pass around. It takes about a week to get print copies in the mail from Create Space.
- You can also choose what paper copy markets you want to get your book into besides the basic Amazon market.

- 'Create Space' also has a link to Kindle Direct Publishing if you want to allow your book to be put onto a Kindle.

- Remember "Scrivener" – it's designed for writers to work on directly and will create the Kindle format for you.

- If you are nervous about tackling any of the single aspects of self-publishing by yourself you can always check out a "You Tube Tutorial" video– how to _____: format a Table of Contents, insert a table into text, insert a photo into text, how to set up footnotes. Whatever you're unsure of.

- You can also get your manuscript on "Mobi" for Amazon. www.mobipocket.com . That app allows you to store all your e books, e news and self-published e documents on your computer. You can download e books in Mobi format from your favorite book store sites to read on your smart phone, your laptop or your desk top. You can add your own published content and documents as well. You can edit metadata (title, author, genre, and publisher) for each title. You can filter, browse, and use the built in search engine to instantly find any e book in your library.

So….

- If you work on your own, make sure your title is ¼ to ½ the cover page. You want people to know what your book is about and for sure who wrote it! You have 100% control over cover and inside art.

- For the back cover of your book you'll want to write a paragraph on what your book is about. Think about what you want your potential readers to know. And make it short and sweet – about 125 words. And don't be tempted to put something that's not true on the back. Fake stuff is sometimes called "Sock puppets", fake reviews that you create when you're just starting out. It is surprising that people make up names of newspapers or literary magazines or professional book reviewers and include this fake information on their back covers. That may come back to bite you big time. However, don't ever pay for reviews. If you're good enough, they'll come to you

- Your author description (the description of yourself) should be written in third person. Again, keep it short and sweet. Basically, just include the pertinent information. That is, the parts of your life that have to do directly with your book topic.

- If you self-publish, a good thing to do might be to set the price low on your first book so people will get hooked on your stories. $2.99 to $10.99 is the sweet spot for online book and e book pricing. If you price your book between these two prices you'll sell more books. 99 cents is the lowest you can price an e book. If you price your e book 99 cents to $2.99 your royalty is 35%. Any higher and your royalty is 25%. Which is still pretty good!

- With self-publishing you have much greater share of the profit. From a book publisher you get 2% of a hardback and 8% of a paperback; that means that you would have to sell about 12,000 paperbacks before you actually begin to make some money. You get about 85 cents for every paperback sold for $7.99 when you go the self-publishing route, which comes to about 10% royalties.

- With self-publishing you get between 25% and 70% of the price of an e book. However, if you self-publish you give up any chance of finding your book in Barnes and Noble

- A gentle reminder: people who don't have entrepreneurial experience, who are shy and retiring, might not want to go this route, because with self-publishing you're on your own for all the legwork, such as publicity and marketing.

- A "story" for Amazon and other online publishers is 8-12,000 words.

- An alternative good way to sell short stories or novellas is one a month for 99 cents; put three together a quarter (year) for $2.99 and at the end of the year do an 'omnibus' of all 12 stories for $9.99 or $10.99.

- You can have Amazon assign you an ISBN # for free. Other publishers charge $100.00 apiece.

- Another site on which you can create, upload, do *and* sell hardbacks is www.lulu.com. It's an online print-on-demand self-publishing and distribution platform. It has printed nearly 2 million copies of various titles in the past several years.

- "Blurb"- www.blurb.com - is another good website for self-publishing. One of its specialties is books with a number of photos, or books with non-traditional formats, like books that include set- off text: recipes or poems, for example. Your book is copyrighted but doesn't have an automatic-assigned anally assigned ISBN number.

- It costs $35.00 to register a copyright with the Library of Congress. Your book is automatically copyrighted as soon as you print it, but if you've copyrighted it and someone steals your stuff, you have more legal basis to sue. (But people who steal your stuff usually wouldn't buy it anyway, so just look at it as free publicity.)

- It can be difficult to get your self-published book into a book store. Example of how a book store handles self-published books: "Local Books Bookstore" takes 40% of the list price of the book. They pay out every six months. After a year you get your unsold books back. You need to follow up on reorders because they won't automatically contact you even if they sell out the first day. So you have to pay attention. It might help if you already have a good relationship with a local bookstore or two, but you need to keep up with your titles and the number you have in a bookstore at any one time. In other words, in this instance you need to be your own business manager.

- For the purposes of self-publishing, or for a publishing company for that matter, what readers like:

  - Adventure stories are usually about 80,000 words.

  - Romances are generally 60,000 words.

  - Thrillers are generally 8-12,000 words.

- Look on www.kindleboards.com –especially its Writers Café - for lots of things. Tips, facts, yellow pages, motivational ideas, children's book editors and other information, just a wealth of useful information of all kinds.

- You might try www.smashwords.com, another online publishing site. It's free to upload your manuscript and it also walks you through the process. It will get your book to small e book sources. Like Amazon and Kindle, you can set your own price and therefore control the royalties you get.

- If you use Amazon to self-publish, "Also boughts" are gold! "Also boughts" are the book titles in the scrolling list below the book someone has just bought, or just looked at. They offer more suggestions for books similar to the one looked at, and your book would look good in that list!

- You might want to check out www.wordpress.com , a site that offers a template for writing that has great flexibility. It also offers web hosting and web site building, as well as how to set up a blog and other kinds of advice for self-publishers.

Last but Not Least: Why Your Title Is Critically Important

You need a really good, accurate title for your work in order for publishers to pay attention to you! Otherwise, if the title doesn't speak to them, they may like your book but not get all the way through it far enough to offer you a contract, so they might toss it.

So you need to really give your potential title some real thought before you settle on one that won't help you.

You need to have your really good title already on your book *before* you send it to an agent or before you contact a publisher.

So make sure your title:

- Reflects your key theme of your story, the key points of your plot, or the key mood surrounding the key points.

- Is worded so that it grabs potential readers right in their emotions.

- Makes someone who picks up the book curious to see what else is inside.

- Is good for marketing your book in now and in the future.

You want someone who walks by the table or the shelf where your book is being sold to be grabbed by the title, enough to stop and look at your book and then pick it up and then buy it.

How do you get to a great title?

- Sit down with yourself and think: brainstorm a list of possible words and/or phrases that you like so far, words that reflect what's on the inside of your book. What do you want most for your readers to take away with them at the end of your book? Remember: brainstorming means you list everything you think of; don't edit yourself yet. Just get all your ideas down first so you can go through them later and narrow down the possibilities.

- Use what teachers call 'picture words.' Those are visual images that your readers will see as soon as they pick up your book.

- Flip through your outline and list words and phrases that jump out at you from anywhere in the outline.

- My suggestion is that you gather at least 25 or so words and phrases. Go for more if you can. A bigger list means more possibilities.

- No go back and start editing. Most agents and publishers like short titles (they are easier for people to remember when they want to look for a good book) so many suggest one noun and one adjective. Go for three or four possibilities.

- Grab a writerly friend, or more than one, and see what she thinks of your choices.

- If you're in a writing group run your possibilities by them.

- Browse through a book store to see how many books in your genre have similar titles to the one you want to use.

- Don't 'create' a title that sounds too much like a well known classic. That will only confuse buyers and won't win you any friends.

- If you have a clever way of looking at life, if you have a clever plot, see if you can make your title as clever as you are.

- Get on the internet just to double check that twelve other books don't have the exact same title you want to use. Unfortunately, if they do you will want to adapt your own title, just to avoid confusion.

- If you want to include a photograph or illustration on your cover make sure it matches your title. And if it isn't of your own making, be sure you have appropriate permissions.

- Remember: shorter is better.

- One other note: once your book gets to a publisher they might very well want to adapt your title to what they think is more appropriate, or they may want to change it completely. Don't cry. At least if you started out with a wonderful title you *got* to a publisher!

Last Tips

- A suggestion: create a Paypal account, separate from your regular checking and savings accounts, which allows you to take credit cards from your own web site. It allows your big publishing company or your self-publishing company to deposit your royalties right into the account. I suggest this separate account just in case – for the sake of security. If you use Amazon you get a royalty payment every month for all the books you've sold that month.

- Also, if you're going your own way, check out www.vistaprint.com or www.shutterfly.com or www.uprint.com, which are web sites that walk you through making your own bookmarks, cards, book bags, stationery, business cards, etc. Especially if you're self-publishing, you'll need to do your own marketing, and those web sites and similar ones are good for little self-marketing tools that you can easily spread around to get your book title out.

- One thing you can do to help yourself market your book is to offer to do workshops or mini workshops for your church, your local Starbucks or other coffee shop, your local senior center, or maybe even a women's shelter.

- You might think about postcards with your book's front cover on them, to use for your notes to friends.

- Get a 7website going to promote your books and to keep your readers up to date on what you're doing.

- If you're good at it create a Facebook page for your books.

- Give your book to the appropriate people for a birthday present, a Christmas present. They will most likely really appreciate it and pass the word.

- Remember: there **is** an audience for your book, even if twenty other people have written books on the same subject. Your perspective is new and different from theirs.

- Think of yourself as a writer all the time.

- Remind yourself periodically that you write your book(s) for the love of writing, not because they will make you rich and famous and retired. Remind yourself that you just love the act of writing.

- Remember: writing is fortunately one of those activities for which you don't need a license or certification or anybody's permission! So don't worry if you don't have fancy credentials. All you need is a good story and the will to get it down on paper.

- So....get started on your next book.

Check Sheet

Before you find yourself going around in circles not knowing what you have or have not finished or what to do next take a long deep breath and see if you can check off the items on this check sheet. You may not need to check off everything but just check the things you think you have done or should have done. This sheet is useful for an organizer, especially if you're new to the writing business. An alternative here is to open a calendar on your computer and get each of these items into it along with the dates you've completed – or started – each step of the process.

1. _____ I've got my descriptions drawn clearly and brightly.

2. _____ I've got the middle of my manuscript tied right to both the beginning and the end.

3. _____ My dialogue is in the right places and is punctuated so it makes sense.

4. _____ I've edited my whole manuscript for continuity and structure.

5. _____ I've contacted a professional editor.

6. _____ I've made arrangements to sign a contract with a professional editor.

7. _____ I've given appropriate credit to others for drawings, artwork, quotations, anything I didn't write myself.

8. _____ I've gotten written permissions from anyone whose work I am including within my manuscript.

9. _____ I've got a plan for a writing group.

10. _____ I've lined up some participants for a writing group.

11. _____ I've written my query letter.

12. _____ I've mailed my query letter.

13. _____ I've written and put together my book proposal (for nonfiction).

14. _____ I've mailed my book proposal to a publisher or agent.

15. _____ I've completed research on which publisher I want to contact.

16. _____ I've contacted an agent.

17. _____ I've arranged to meet an agent.

18. _____ I've signed a contract with an agent.

19. _____ I know what galleys are and can proof them myself.

20. _____ I've got a great title!

21. _____ I've decided to go with a self-publishing program.

22. _____ I've got my cover art decided/done/contracted.

23. _____ I've got footnotes in the right places, or I've got end notes organized.

24. _____ I've got a table of contents completed.

25. _____ I've got my 'About the Author' blurb completed.

26. _____ I've got my back of book blurb completed.

27. _____ I am ready to go!

About the Author:

Kathy Tuten has been an educator for more than four decades. She was a middle school English teacher, writing teacher, newspaper sponsor, creative writing teacher, and literary magazine editor. She was an assistant principal, principal and a school system level instructional officer, as well as a state and national level leadership program creator and director, at the University of North Carolina – Chapel Hill, and for the State of South Carolina and the state of Massachusetts.

She taught Freshman Composition 101 at the University of North Carolina-Charlotte.

Kathy was one of the first 25 Fellows in the Bay Area Writing Project when it first moved from the San Francisco Bay Area and went national.

Kathy has conducted seminars on teaching writing at the middle and high school levels throughout the Southeast for the past 30 years, working with teachers to encourage and foster student writing skills on a broad level.

Kathy teaches writing classes at the local Senior Center on a quarterly basis and has several writers with manuscripts ready for publication. She also does professional editing for those whose manuscripts are all but ready to go to a publisher or to be self-published.

Kathy has a B.A. in English from Pennsylvania State University, an M.ED. in Education from the University of North Carolina, Curriculum Specialist Certification, Supervision, and Advanced Administrative Certification from The University of North Carolina, and has pursued post-graduate studies at the University of North Carolina.

If you need some 'real person' help e mail her at k.tuten@live.com .